SYMBOLISM IN RELIGION AND ART

Charles Thomas Taylor

University Press of America,® Inc.
Lanham · Boulder · New York · Toronto · Plymouth, UK

Copyright © 2008 by
University Press of America,® Inc.
4501 Forbes Boulevard
Suite 200
Lanham, Maryland 20706
UPA Acquisitions Department (301) 459-3366

Estover Road
Plymouth PL6 7PY
United Kingdom

Library of Congress Control Number: 2007933449
ISBN-13: 978-0-7618-3875-3 (paperback : alk. paper)
ISBN-10: 0-7618-3875-9 (paperback : alk. paper)

CONTENTS

PREFACE

All of my prior thought (expressed in four published books) has focused on two major concerns: to affirm and to defend empiricism in epistemology; and to identify and to develop an appropriate and effective ethics for the improvement of human life everywhere. These earlier efforts led me to explore the three primary arenas of human concern and activity: politics, economics and religion. While I was able to identify political and economic ideologies that are compatible with my ethical conclusions, I felt a strong need to make a further attempt to settle some lingering questions in the area of religion. At the same time, I continued to nurture a strong desire to reconcile (if not to integrate) my two most powerful lifelong interests, music and philosophy, by writing a book on aesthetics. The present project represents the outcome of an effort to satisfy both of these personal needs.

The discussion of the presence, use and interpretation of symbolism in both religion and art is, of course, that which unifies two seemingly unrelated topics. Throughout the book, I attempt to demonstrate that—in either area—symbolism communicates *ethical* value. Unable to abandon ethics in any serious discussion of religion or art, I quickly discovered that neither could I abandon empiricism. Accordingly, the book attempts to reconcile the apparent and historical contradiction between utility and beauty by pointing out the distinction between real and imaginary experience. Since the perceiver's appreciation of beauty, whether in nature or art, does not subvert his or her exercise of reason, the experience of beauty is generally applauded. By the same token, the book is unable to be as kind with regard to the experience of the supernatural in religion. Since, under empiricism, much of religion is irrational and, in certain instances, even antirational, the book can neither support nor even condone the perseverance of religion in human experience. The prologue introduces this approbation of art but disapprobation of religion as the central premise of the book.

Although *Symbolism in Religion and Art* may be seen to offer some new and original ideas in either sphere of human activity—such as the evolution of the concept of God in religion and the symbolic representations of effective work or of amiable interpersonal relations in absolute music—it is essentially a work of philosophy or anthropology that attempts either to integrate or not to integrate, as the case may be, the peripheral concerns of religion and aesthetics with a central ethical vision for the future of our species.

I wish to thank Marie Ajour and Dana Mendell for their indispensable assistance during the course of preparing my manuscript for publication.

Charles Thomas Taylor
Denver, Colorado; April, 2007

PROLOGUE

When a baby is born, it instinctively seeks the breast of its mother and sucks at the nipple to regain the nourishment it can no longer draw from a severed umbilical cord. The baby continues to receive its nourishment in this manner until the day comes when it can be weaned from its mother because it has begun to eat from a spoon and to drink from a cup. From this time forward, the baby gradually becomes aware that the source of its nourishment lies outside of the body of its mother.

As it grows older, the same child may be given a stuffed animal or a doll to serve as a surrogate for a family member or a playmate and to provide a feeling of security and contentment when the child is left alone, as when just before falling asleep or upon awakening. The child sometimes recognizes that the toy is not real (that is, that it is not a living being) but at other times the child imagines that it *is* and by doing so revives the feeling of happiness that had been initially aroused upon the introduction of the toy. When the child becomes an adult and no longer takes interest in the toys of childhood, he or she may still find delight in the portrait or the photograph of a loved one even if the child-become-adult may be separated, either temporarily or permanently, from the person represented in the picture.

We can see that in the opening period of the life of a human being, the individual is interacting with his or her environment at the most rudimentary levels of consciousness—first, at the level of urges and sensations, of instinct and will; next, at the level of the emotions; then, of conceptualization; and finally, of imagination. In the foregoing observations, we can see that the newborn is interacting both with things and with states—with himself or herself, with nourishment, with objects, with other living beings, with companionship. In the beginning, the baby is only aware of itself and of nourishment. It identifies its mother both with itself and with nourishment. Gradually, as the baby becomes aware of its mother as a separate person, it begins to conceptualize such that the person of its mother becomes a symbol for nourishment. With the further passage of time, the toddler becomes able to differentiate between the most simple of things and states. The toddler's ability to conceptualize also so improves that things the initial perceptions of which had never been misapprehended as an identity with the self are presently available to serve as symbols for still other things or states. Thus, the stuffed animal or the doll is able to become a symbol for companionship. We can see, then, that each child interacts with an inanimate object or another living being either as an object or a being in itself or as a symbol of some other object, being, or state, or both as an object or a being in itself and as a symbol of some other object, being, or state.

At the dawn of the era of man, there must have been but few and minor anatomical and behavioral differences between the members of our own species and those of the other genera and species (all now extinct) from which we evolved. Paleontological evidence confirms that at least one of these now extinct species, Neanderthal man, was briefly coterminous with the period of the onset of one of the earliest representatives of our own species, Cro-Magnon man. Paleontology also provides strong support for the hypothesis that Hominidae, the zoological family of man, evolved over 500,000 years ago (and perhaps even up to five or ten million years ago) from the older, less developed forms of life through Pongidae, the family of the great apes. Now, like all life-forms, man is subject to the seven-fold law of nature which requires of each organism that it (1) secures sufficient food and water to sustain its internal energy; (2) protects itself against predators; (3) successfully competes with other organisms in the quest for food and water; (4) reproduces individuals of its own kind; (5) grows to maturity and heals after injury or illness; (6) responds to external stimuli (as in a vital reaction to its physiological urges and physical sensations of pleasure and comfort or discomfort and pain); and (7) excretes the wastes of its own body. With his more highly-developed mind, which included among its various capacities not only ones for perception, cognition, recognition, memory, emotion, reflex, and volition but also others for imagination and reason, man was soon able to surpass the lower life-forms in satisfying the demanding requirements of the law of nature. The lengthy process during which man, by virtue of reason, became able within his own biosphere not only to contend with nature but ultimately, to a considerable extent, to modify it and to control it—not only for his own sake but for the improvement of nature itself—can quite aptly be described as the period of the contemporaneousness of the law of nature and the law of reason, the full expression of the latter generally lying at rest, as it were, as an embryo in the collective womb of an emerging species.

Since he first emerged from the apes, man has distinguished himself from the other animals by his deliberate and habitual use of tools. With the invention of weapons, this advancement in his behavior enabled man to overcome and eventually to eliminate his predators, effectively reducing the magnitude of the laws of nature (with respect to himself) from seven to six. The original substances from which many of the early tools were fashioned included stone, wood, bone, antler, and ivory, and since the most commonly-used substance was stone, the Tool Age of the cultural development of man has generally been referred to as the Stone Age, further divided into the Paleolithic (the old Stone Age, characterized by the use of rough or chipped stone implements) and the Neolithic (the New Stone Age, characterized by the use of polished stone implements), the two divisions separated by a transitional period, the Mesolithic (the Middle Stone Age) and the second division followed in turn by two increasingly more highly-advanced periods, the Bronze Age and the Iron Age.

By the onset of the Bronze Age, the cultural development of man had progressed from primeval societies that may best be described as hunter-gatherer to ones that were pastoral-nomadic and finally to ones that were fixed settlement-agricultural. Those among the latter category that were favorably located along the banks of the great rivers of the tropical and subtropical zones of the Eastern Hemisphere developed into the great civilizations of antiquity—Egypt, Mesopotamia, the Indus Civilization of ancient India, and the Yellow River Civilization of ancient China. Knowledge and technology flourished with the development of civilization—the invention of writing, of the wheel and the plow, and of basic machines such as the screw, the windlass, the pulley, the pump, and the inclined plane; the development of agriculture, astronomy, engineering, and architecture with related trades such as carpentry, masonry, milling, brewing, baking, tanning, and weaving; and the introduction of education, of a formal methodology for the acquisition of knowledge, and of abstract study in such fields as mathematics, logic, and rhetoric.

Knowledge and technology progressed slowly and gradually after the dawn of civilization, moving forward dramatically in certain places such as ancient Greece while suffering inertia or setback elsewhere. Then, after the passage of several centuries of sporadic progress, the Renaissance erupted in Western Europe during the fifteen and sixteenth centuries, giving rise to the Scientific Revolution of the seventeenth and eighteenth centuries. The Scientific Revolution crystallized in England with the publication of Isaac Newton's *Principia*, 1687, and John Locke's *Essay Concerning Human Understanding*, 1690, and it later precipitated the Industrial Revolution of the nineteenth and twentieth centuries. With the outset of the Industrial Revolution, the Tool Age of the cultural history of mankind quickly transformed into the Machine Age. The inauguration and subsequent rapid ascendence of the age of the law of reason was the beneficial effect of the Renaissance and the Scientific Revolution. Now, one of the two forms and manifestations of the ascendence of the law of reason in modern history has been the rapid ascendence and globalization of scientific technology. The Industrial Revolution has diffused beyond Europe and North America to reach and to affect all parts of the world, providing the greater portion of mankind with the basic necessities of life while liberating the same from the burden of manual labor. With the ascendence and globalization of scientific technology over the past three hundred years, man has finally become able to overcome all of nature except for himself. Through the remaining form and manifestation of the ascendence of the law of reason, man also has finally become able to become master of himself.

We are now speaking of the ascendence of universalism over particularism, which is to say that man, as a rational animal (to use Aristotle's definition), has finally attained full self-awareness. Each person has come to recognize that he, or she, is fundamentally no different than every other person; that he, or she, is but a member of the rational species; and that he, or she, cannot achieve lasting personal happiness in the absence of interpersonal respect, goodwill, and justice. But this acknowledgement flies in the face of the vestiges of natural aggression in a heretofore primitive life-form. Accordingly, it is only through the effective and sufficient exercise of his reason that man can finally and permanently overcome all that he shares in common with all of the other animals, all that which in the past has prevented and which, if not suppressed and sublimed in the future, can only continue to prevent his attainment of continuous and lasting personal happiness.

The ascendence of universalism over particularism arose coincidentally with the ascendence and globalization of scientific technology at the close of the seventeenth century. Even as the aforementioned works of Newton and Locke were critically instrumental in the genesis of the latter phenomenon, so the publication of Locke's *Two Treatises of Government* in 1690 (and particularly the translation from English into French of the second treatise with its subsequent reverse translation from French back into English for dissemination in the American colonies) along with the publication of the *Essay Concerning Human Understanding* were similarly catalytic in the genesis of the former.

The inevitable consequence of the ascendence of the universal over the particular is nothing other than the ascendence of democracy in politics and of capitalism in economics. The latter proceeds from the former with little or no difficulty but the former must engender eventually coincidental processes of national democratization and world federalization. Once a world democratic federal government has been inaugurated, a common body of international law can also be established to serve as the social contract for a unified species. Ultimately, a unified world will require a common morality constructed upon a rational foundation. Such a morality can certainly be formulated by drawing together the rational elements of the existing major moral codes of the world. Once the relevant processes for the ascendence of the universal over the particular have been established, developed, and fulfilled, man will at last be able to achieve lasting personal happiness. He need then be concerned only with attaining as much personal happiness as may be possible within the permanent and unalterable limitations imposed by nature.

There is no question that nature has provided man with the means to know when he is being successful in his attempts to fulfill the requirements for survival. In the oft-quoted words of Jeremy Bentham from the opening two sentences of *The Principles of Morals and Legislation* (1781), "Nature has placed mankind under the governance of two sovereign masters, pain and pleasure. It is for them alone to point out what we ought to do, as well as to determine what we shall do." Bentham is correct in acknowledging one of the elementary principles of the science of psychology and in then predicating a valid and complete system of moral philosophy upon this principle. This moral philosophy, utilitarianism, may be thought of as a kind of refined and improved form of Epicureanism, just as Epicureanism is but a kind of refined and improved form of hedonism. It is natural and self-evident that we should accept, even seek, pleasure and reject pain, but to understand the uneasy development of the moral philosophy flowing from our natural desires and aversions, we must consider two hypothetical situations. First, we recognize that a little or a moderate degree of pleasure over a given period of time is generally good but that an excess of pleasure often leads to pain, while a little discomfort is generally valuable for us to indicate the onset of a problem which, if left uncorrected, may progress to successive conditions of malaise, pain, infirmity, disability, and, ultimately, even death. (This phenomenon, normal but not necessarily absolute, betrays persons who suffer from drug addiction, in that they possess no intrinsic physiological mechanism to signal immediate and increasing discomfort, albeit a discomfort that is concurrent with a pleasurable effect, when they are ingesting too large a quantity of an intoxicating substance.) Second, we learn too often with the greatest difficulty that when we seek personal comfort, pleasure, and happiness while simultaneously we attempt to avoid or to alleviate personal distress, pain, and misfortune, either to the deliberate detriment of others or with little or no consideration for the well-being of others, our immediate happiness and security generally and gradually, or sometimes even abruptly, gives way to a new phenomenon of pain and distress. (For example, let us simply recall the last days of the monarchies of France and Russia.) Accordingly, any moral idea that is perceived as natural, simple, and self-evident ultimately requires a rational, complex, and thoughtful formulation.

All organisms strive to satisfy the requirements of the law of nature until, ultimately, nature betrays the organism and the organism decays and dies. Nature is indifferent with respect to the quantitative and qualitative attributes of life but man cannot be indifferent to the same since no one, under normal circumstances, desires to die prematurely or to experience pain either during life or at death. For man, all collective efforts for the effective satisfaction of the requirements of the law of nature can be exclusively supported by that which is presently reducible to but two rational instrumentalities. The first is technological and it is responsible for providing the resources to meet the necessities of life—food, water, clothing, and shelter—and to assist and to improve such natural processes as reproduction, growth, and healing. (This technological instrumentality includes a cultural component which provides education, enables the construction of societal infrastructure, and supports theoretical science and technological innovation.) The second is ethical and it is responsible for attaining and sustaining the optimal equilibrium between competition and cooperation. Either instrumentality is insufficient without the other and inasmuch as morality is presently absent, neglected, or predicated upon irrational foundations throughout the greater portion of the world while a universal morality predicated solely upon reason is present only as potentiality, man survives in an unsatisfactory and precarious condition that is likely to become increasingly unsatisfactory and precarious in the future should technology begin to falter and a singular morality for the benefit of all sentient beings fail to ascend and to globalize.

As individuals, we are all aware of the various ways that we typically set about to satisfy the requirements of life. Over the course of a lifetime, we obtain an education, secure a livelihood, find a mate, raise a family, look after our health, save for retirement, and so on. In our daily cycles, we enjoy sensual pleasure, or relieve physiological tension and emotional anxiety, by eating meals, by drinking alcoholic beverages, and by gratifying our sexual urges with our mates. We derive emotional satisfaction from our work, from socialization, from our achievements, and from any honors flowing from our achievements—in short, we find enduring happiness beyond our immediate pleasures both in our personal achievements and in our interpersonal relationships. All of these sources of pleasure and happiness involve the engagement of one or another of the various capacities of the human mind. For example, we engage our memory when, a day (or perhaps after, or even over, a number of days) later, we recall with a certain kind of pleasure a particularly satisfying meal or a social event (as a commencement or an awards ceremony) held in recognition (whether in full or even if only in part) of our personal achievements. Furthermore, we engage our imagination on two generally discrete occasions—one, when we relieve anxiety by finding hope and courage in religion and, two, when we increase our happiness by taking delight in beauty, whether that of nature or of art. Let us pause for a moment to discuss briefly each of these satisfactions deriving from the imagination.

The origin of man within the evolution of life on earth is largely concealed in temporal remoteness and the beginnings of his cultural development, of course, are even more obscure. Like the lower forms of animals from which he evolved, man certainly was constantly obliged to satisfy the obvious requirements of the law of nature and otherwise to contend with erratic natural forces for his very survival but unlike the other animals, man came to possess a more highly-developed brain which allowed him to attain, to enjoy, and to develop an unprecedented capacity to think beyond the most rudimentary and localized levels of zoological thought. With improved thought came reflection, which certainly must have occurred back then (as of course it does today) during the brief periods of rest or inactivity immediately following those occasions when man temporarily satisfied his natural urges (such as feasts, sexual intercourse, and sleep), and man certainly came to recognize that his struggle against nature was quite difficult, that his continual success was generally uncertain, and that the prognosis for his permanent existence was most improbable, and consequently he came to envision a state of human existence free from the forces of nature and from all of the exacting demands of the law of nature, in other words, a supernatural state of being. (Let us recall that the supernatural essentially is that which is of, or which relates to, an order of existence beyond the visible observable universe, which is to admit that the supernatural is nonempirical by definition and is, at best, only latently hypothetical.) Man also developed an abiding interest—at once a highly imaginative and emotional albeit irrational interest—

in the supernatural, both as an ultimate source of superhuman assistance in coping with the immediate dangers and demands of nature and as an eventual destination for permanent existence. Man then almost certainly invented religion as the means of gaining access to the supernatural.

We have already stated that man's interest in the supernatural was more emotional than rational. Why should we have said so? Because we have been unable not to surmise that man quickly recognized the true nature of his own existence: an existence filled with enormous difficulties and uncertainties in the course of attaining but few, albeit generally intense, pleasures; an existence continually punctuated by pain and fatigue; and an existence always culminating in death. Yet man's advanced mental faculties surely allowed him to develop a propensity to remember and to anticipate his pleasures and to forget or to repress the memory of his pains. This propensity, which may be designated by the term "human optimism," became the foundation for the possibility of human happiness.

We should digress to note that the sensation of pleasure arises from the effective satisfaction of a natural urge or a related need, while the effective assuagement of the sensation of pain, in the course of restoring a human organism from a sensation of pain to that brief state of an absence of sensation, gives rise to a sensation that is somewhat analogous to pleasure. Happiness, then, is no more than a conscious instantaneous reflection upon the sensations that are engendered by the satisfaction of urges, drives, and needs as well as the assuagement of pain and/or the avoidance or elimination of potential sources of pain. The presence of the sensation of pleasure, which is prolonged through the presence of the emotion of happiness that arises upon reflection, with the absence of both the sensation of pain and the related emotion of misery, certainly is that which provides original, passing, and ultimate (or, in a word, constant) meaning for human existence.

Since a particular sensation and a particular emotion provide meaning for human existence, all of the remaining faculties of the human mind are quickly pressed into service, usually indiscriminately, in the effort to attain and/or to sustain pleasure and happiness. While reason certainly is the highest of the mental faculties, it is not among those which directly provide meaning for life and it can function only as a means to the desired end. In this respect, it must assume its essential role as the governing faculty of the intellect. Hitherto, the role of reason in the pursuit of pleasure and happiness has been largely overlooked or trivialized. However, without reason, human happiness is only accidental or illusory. Now, human optimism clearly is somewhat irrational. Yet this is neither to infer nor to suggest that human optimism is an unworthy foundation for human happiness since the presence of optimism clearly is conducive to happiness and most probably is more beneficial for human existence than either the presence of pessimism or even (if such might be possible) an emotionally-detached absence of both optimism and pessimism. This is only to advocate that optimism must always be tempered by reason.

Man has never been able to affirm the existence of the supernatural through his reason, yet the possibility of the existence of the supernatural persists in his imagination. Accordingly, all of the religions of mankind have been predicated upon an unconfirmed and increasingly improbable working hypothesis. In the mysterious domain of religion, imagination lies much closer to emotion than to reason, which is why most people will be ready to admit, should they be questioned about their religious attitudes and beliefs, to a kind of statement such as this: "I generally don't fully understand the true nature or ultimate end of reality as it has been presented to me in religion; I simply know that religion seems to help me to cope with the difficulties of life in the present and to find hope for a happy and permanent existence in the future."

Now, let us turn our attention to another use of the imagination. When we perceive beauty, whether we are looking at a snowcapped mountain, a lovely flower, or an attractive person, or whether we are reading a novel, watching a play, or listening to a symphony, we increase our pleasure and happiness through a vicarious experience. Now, the direct sources of pleasure are the immediate satisfaction of our natural urges, such as by eating and drinking or by indulging in sexual gratification, or the immediate assuagements of our sporadic hurts, and the direct sources of happiness include our reflection upon such pleasures, our engagement in useful activities to acquire the resources for meeting the necessities of life, and our involvement in beneficial relationships with other people for accomplishing shared objectives. The effective and habitual satisfaction of our needs, with the equally effective and timely mitigation of our hurts, or the avoidance or repulsion of whatever may tend to hurt us, provide us with a sense of order and a feeling of confidence in our lives. Through the perception of beauty, we recapture or intensify this feeling of confidence and sense of order, depending upon whether we perceive such beauty at the same times that we are satisfying our needs, assuaging our hurts, or reflecting on the same, or at different times. This mental connection between the order which we seek in our personal lives and the order which we perceive in the beauty of the world is achieved through symbolism. We will attempt to speak to this poorly-understood phenomenon with greater clarification and some degree of analysis in due course. Most people, of course, remain largely unaware of why they are so deeply affected by beauty and will simply dismiss the question by answering something like this: "I most often don't really understand why I like a particular object of natural or artistic beauty, I just know that I like it."

Moments of perfection in human experience are rare. Symbolism in religion and art integrates human experience with imaginary perfection. The two phenomena differ as follows. Symbolism in art integrates that which is imperfect with that which is perfect in the here and now, that is, in the present world. Symbolism in religion integrates that which is imperfect in the here and now with that which is perfect in the there and then, that is, it integrates that which is imperfect in the present world with that which is perfect, whether entirely outside of the world, or deep into the future of the world, or both. The one increases a happiness that is already present, the other seeks a happiness that is not present but that is only potential. The one readily embraces present human reality, the other simply endures it.

Let us be clear that in our evaluation of the merit or the lack of merit of beauty or religion, we are never taking issue with symbolism per se since symbolism is merely the vehicle by which we comprehend and communicate perfection in human experience. Rather, we are taking issue with (where we may not have otherwise already fully accepted, whether unconditionally or conditionally) the experience of beauty or the experience of religion.

When we satisfy our needs and avert our hurts, we experience pleasure; consequent reflection on the same gives rise to happiness. As we satisfy our needs and avert our hurts, our experience of beauty (whether incidental or intentional) increases our pleasure; consequent reflection on the same increases our happiness. When we fail to satisfy our needs and to avert our hurts, our experience of beauty, if it should occur at all, is most likely to be incidental and not intentional but it may eventuate to be our only source of pleasure during that time of difficulty. We may conclude, then, that everyone and everything that is conducive to the experience of beauty, artistic as well as natural, is always good and desirable—not as a substitute for but as a supplement to all that is instrumental for the satisfaction of our needs and the aversion of our hurts. The perception and cognition of natural and artistic beauty supplements and reinforces our most elemental pleasure and happiness.

As members of the human species, our efforts to satisfy needs and to avert hurts require reason. Our efforts require work, supported by an effective technology, and cooperation, supported by an appropriate ethics. Through reason, we fully satisfy our needs and avert our hurts, we master all of nature—including our own selves—that has any relevance for human existence, and we achieve pleasure and happiness. On the other hand, religious experience attempts to enable us to gain access to the supernatural, which we are unable to perceive and which is most unlikely even to exist. Accordingly, the supernatural is fundamentally irrational. To the extent that religion, as the vehicle for something that is fundamentally irrational, tends to denigrate and to detract from our efforts to satisfy the requirements of our existence, it is antirational. But religion has persisted to this day not so much because we may still believe, like our primeval ancestors, that we must rely upon supernatural assistance for survival as because we imagine that we can continue to exist after we die (because we have become so attached to life notwithstanding our recognition that all that lives must die, which is to say, that desire is stronger than reason). The human species has retained two primitive qualities from its natural heritage that it has been unable to control or even to ignore without the greatest of difficulties—an entrenched propensity for aggression and a latent capacity for self-deception. As long as we succeed in satisfying our needs and averting our hurts, we can entertain religion in the hope of attaining eternal life. We must argue, however, that religion has become an illusory and injurious diversion from rational endeavor, that it does little to enable us to meet the obvious requirements for survival, and that, as a social institution, it distrusts, spurns, and discourages our best attempts to envision and to build a better world. Many will maintain that religion has also persisted because it functions as the primary vehicle for the transmittal of ethics but I have argued elsewhere (hopefully with an effectual measure of success) that the moral foundation for a unified species must be in and of itself but one dimension of the rational foundation of a unified world such as must be, by its own definition, fully independent of the domain of religion. Unlike the perceptions of beauty, which give rise to so many pleasant emotional experiences (generally involving a subconscious rational ordering of natural or artificial phenomena), the practices of religion entail the pursuit of objectives that are fundamentally antirational and useless although such practices sometimes appear to give rise to consolatory emotional experiences. We must conclude, then, that the experience of religion is generally neither good nor desirable and ought to be abandoned as quickly as possible since it is not predicated upon truth and, as a consequence, it most often creates more injury than nurture. But others will ask, in the spirit of Pascal and with the memory of his famous wager, "May religion not be retained for the comfort of all of those closest to death—for the very old, the gravely ill, and those who live or work under conditions of extreme hardship and danger?" And we could reply, "Perhaps, but only to create happiness through a contained illusion, as when we encourage our young children to believe in Santa Claus or when we humor those who are mentally ill." We might easily defend such a reply with the words of Pascal: "The heart has its reasons which reason does not know." However, we know that we would do much better if we were always to uphold the primacy of truth under all circumstances, even those of impending death. Let us imagine a world of reason in which dangerous conditions will have been eliminated, diseases will have been cured, premature death will no longer occur, and people will have learned neither to injure nor to abuse themselves or others, or any other sentient beings, or the very biosphere upon which all life forms depend. In such a world, people will certainly live long and happy lives, will experience neither pain nor misery, and will die as a consequence of old age and, even then, without pain. Even as everyone, in the course of personal daily experience, eventually becomes aware of the intensity associated with the earlier part of the day vis-à-vis the relaxation associated with the later, so may everyone in such a world also come by degrees to recognize the robust energy of youth vis-à-vis the sweet fatigue of old age so that the gradual and inevitable progress of each life will continuously engender the immediate source of its own natural satisfaction and fulfillment. Accordingly, no one will continue to desire either eternal life or a recurrence of life but each one will desire merely to live one's own life to its natural limit. In such a world, the doctrine of the mean, central to the ethics of the golden ages of ancient Greece and China, will have at last become applicable to human existence itself: deficiency—the life cut short; excess—life without end; the Golden Mean—a long and happy life lived through flood and ebb to its natural conclusion. In such a world, religion will have lost all of its past and present value and will neither need to be practiced nor remembered. In such a world, religion will have finally become obsolete.

If we can truly accept that which we have just suggested: that, within an ethical perspective over a far-extended future, art may abide but religion must perish, we would surely prefer to be content with that much and not deliberately to expose ourselves to the possibility of recriminations for presuming to predict the time and place for the death of a fantasy. At this early point in our discussion, we might even concede that religion may endure for as long as it will, or for as long as people give it leave, provided that it can be perceived neither to impede rational endeavor nor to cause obvious injury to humankind, to other sentient beings, or to the biosphere.

Our discussion of imaginary perfection within human experience comprises two principal discourses: one in the philosophy of religion, the other in aesthetics. In the first of these, which directly follows, we will explore the rich use of symbolism in religion and how it tends to reveal the preeminent concerns of man, speaking more to the evolution of a species than to an ultimate reality of existence.

PART ONE—SYMBOLISM IN RELIGION

From the time that one species of life differentiated itself from all of the others (by exhibiting the capacity to think) emerged the original understanding of human existence within the natural biosphere. We must bear in mind that our primordial ancestors who first appeared sometime between one and ten million years ago almost certainly behaved more like apes than like later human beings (such as we might have expected to find them if we could have been there with them at the dawn of civilization some five or six thousand years ago) but unlike the apes, primitive man was unable not to be aware that his life was at once a stream of isolated moments of intense pleasure and an incessant struggle against nature attended by pain, violence, injury, and sickness. With little or no social organization above the level of the family, our primordial ancestors surely spent their days in searching for food: gathering leaves, bark, seeds, fruits, nuts, roots, insects, mollusks, and crustaceans; catching birds and fish; and hunting and trapping animals for meat. Besides possessing a more highly developed brain, our ancestors, like the other primates, possessed certain other highly specialized anatomical adaptations, including stereoscopic binocular vision with refined depth perception, and hands with jointed fingers and a thumb rotating in opposition to the other fingers to permit a precision grip. Like the other primates, our ancestors certainly used tools, such as in using rocks to smash coconuts, or sticks to probe for termites, or in curving the palm of the hand (or the joined palms of both hands) to ladle water for drinking and washing, but unlike the other primates, our ancestors also learned to make tools, using stone, wood, shells, bones, antlers, sinews, feathers, and other natural materials. The earliest man-made tools included hammers, scrapers, sweepers, axes, and drills. Besides making and using tools to procure and to prepare food, to fashion clothing, and to build shelter, our ancestors learned sometime to make and to use fire for frightening away predatory animals, for lighting and heating shelters, and for cooking food. Yet for all of his progress (which, of course, was the obvious effect of the willful employment of his reason), primitive man was never able to ignore his awareness of his ever precarious condition, of his inescapable vulnerability to disease, of the inevitable debilitation associated with his aging, and of the constant danger of suffering injury from the aggression of predators and enemies. Of even greater consequence, primitive man was unable not to be aware that his life was finite inasmuch as death, over and above nonfatal injury, was all around him. He encountered death in the missteps that lead to accidents, in the ravages of disease, in prolonged exposure to the elements, in natural disasters, in the lethal attacks of predators and enemies, and, at times, even as a consequence of the aberrational, irrational, and irresponsible activities of relatives and friends. With a constant awareness of the difficulties of human life in the natural world and of the inevitability of death, primitive man turned to his imagination for comfort. He created for himself a possibility, however improbable and implausible, and consequently a hope, both for superhuman assistance in his epic struggle against the forces of nature and for a supernatural destination for the continuation of his life at the moment of his natural death—which is to say, that he created a world of spirits, of immortal supernatural beings, in and of a place and time apart from his physical environment, in and of that place and time of an almost fully unfathomable there and then.

In the earliest stages of cultural development, human beings most likely conceived of spiritual beings as little removed from the here and now. Spirits almost certainly must have been seen either as friends or enemies—as friends, if they were seen to provide help in satisfying the requirements of human existence or in averting or alleviating the injuries of life; as enemies, if they were regarded as instrumental in frustrating, whether in whole or in part, human efforts to satisfy the requirements of life or to avert or to alleviate human hurts. Accordingly, primitive man most likely would have attempted to attract and to secure the assistance of all available friendly spirits so as to assure success in human endeavors; conversely, he would have attempted to propitiate any hostile spirits so as to prevent their interference in human affairs. Furthermore, those phenomena of natural energy that were most obvious and familiar to primitive man—thunder and lightning, intense storms, fire, stampedes, earthquakes, floods, volcanic eruptions, the ebb and flow of tidal waters, the violence of carnivorous predators, and human violence—quite likely would have been attributed to the presence, activity, and influence of supernatural beings.

In fairness to the developing mental processes of our primordial ancestors, we should not conclude that man's original belief in supernatural beings was a result at once of the full abandonment of reason and of the full engagement of imagination: man most likely arrived at his belief in the supernatural world through a significant exercise of his reason, albeit with faulty consequences, in addition to a fruitful engagement of his imagination. Let us digress for a moment to consider how this may have happened.

Primitive man most likely and most easily must have had to have associated life with things that move, that is, with human beings, with all other species of animals that exhibit movement, and even with such natural phenomena as wind, fire, and moving water. Primitive man also most likely must have had to have noticed that movement appears almost entirely to cease during sleep, only to return upon awakening. When he observed that a person had died, under certain circumstances, as when the body remained intact with no obvious signs of injury, he may have likened the death to a long and deep sleep, particularly if he had previously become aware of the hibernation of various species of animals during the seasons of cold weather. When primitive man observed some of his fellows, or some other animals, sleeping, it is most likely that he imagined that their spirits—that part of their being that was believed either to move or otherwise to cause movement—were somehow away, in a different place altogether, albeit in a place most likely envisaged not all that far away from the immediate location. Then when he observed death, he likewise imagined that the spirit had left the body and gone away, possibly to return to the body at a later time, possibly to take up residence in another natural object, where it would animate that object and give it movement, and, in either event, possibly to occupy some supernatural location during the interim. Thus, primitive man most likely conceived the transmigration of spirits. Also, inasmuch as human beings, like the other primates, had come to attain a relatively advanced degree of communication between individuals of the species, primitive man most likely attempted to communicate not only with his fellows but with the other beings and natural objects with which he associated life (that is, as we have said, with things that move or function otherwise as an agent of movement). Thus, primitive man most likely attempted to communicate with spirits, whether such spirits (or their surmised effects) should be visible or not.

With respect to plants, it is not very likely that primitive man associated life with them at all, inasmuch as plants generally do not exhibit obvious movement. Therefore, he would have noticed little or no difference between a living tree and one that had died from disease or a strike of lightning, provided that the dead tree was still standing and that its appearance was the same as, or little different from, that of the living tree.

Now, our primordial ancestors most likely were at first culturally organized as hunter-gatherers (with a strict separation of function by gender) and, from our understanding of existing Paleolithic societies, we can deduce not only that the "hunting," generally performed by men, was taken up so as to find and to kill animals for food while the "gathering," predominantly an activity of women, involved collecting various kinds of plants to eat, but that early man's belief in the power and influence of supernatural beings was at that time primarily associated with hunting, and not with gathering, since primitive man associated life (and, as a consequence, spirits) only with things that move.

We would concur with the conclusions of the English anthropologist Edward B. Tylor, who postulated in his book *Primitive Culture* (1871) that the first religion (which he designated by the term "animism") emerged as "the general belief in spiritual beings." There were probably numerous ways in which animism became manifest throughout the primeval world, some of which, such as shamanism and totemism, have persisted to the present and are still evident among certain primitive tribes, including the Dayak of Borneo and the Haida of British Columbia and Alaska.

When primeval man was essentially a hunter-gatherer, his spatial dimensions varied considerably while his temporal dimension remained fixed in the present moment. As time passed, some hunter-gatherer societies settled at fixed locations to become agricultural communities. Once this level of cultural development had been attained, man's temporal dimensions widened even as his spatial dimensions narrowed. By this time, man had come to see things beyond the present moment, to become aware that plants are also a form of life, and to recognize the life cycle of birth, growth, maturity, decay, and death. By this time, the orbit of man's spiritual world also had expanded. No longer exclusively a world of innumerable animal and human spirits inhabiting the human biosphere or a supernatural domain in close proximity, the spiritual world also embraced the gods and goddesses of the earth or fertility, of the sky, sun, and moon, and of the rivers and rain—in short, a small and select number of supernatural beings of increased stature, whose imagined relevance for successful human endeavor had abruptly increased, and the members of the most exalted portion of which were held to reside in an ideal location far-removed from the natural world. As man steadily began to conceive of a kind of hierarchy of such spiritual beings, with the greater spiritual beings residing in mystical locations exceedingly remote from the locations of the lesser spiritual beings residing on or close to the earth, he also almost certainly began to conceive either of an afterlife in a perfect and blissful supernatural domain or otherwise of an ultimate and permanent liberation from a recurring cycle of earthly transmigrations.

At about this same time, in association with his first thoughts on a better way to be and a better place to be in, man at last and for once began to think about the origin of all that is, including, in particular, that of himself. Most of the diverse ancient mythologies of which we have knowledge (including Egyptian, Babylonian, Hebrew, Buddhist, Siberian, Oceanian, African, North American Indian, and South American Indian myths) assert that, from the beginning, there was only water. Then the earth emerged out of a stone or a clamshell thrown or dropped into the original water. The mythologies of the ancient Middle East relate the existence of an original group of basic gods and goddesses which gave birth to a number of less primitive gods and goddesses, which, in turn, killed or banished the original gods and goddesses while either giving birth to human beings or otherwise creating them out of clay, stone, earth, or the body parts of the slain original gods and goddesses.

I would now postulate that there is convincing evidence to indicate an evolution in human thought (over and above the well-established and widely recognized empirical evidence in support of the evolution of life) when we consider the rather late origin of the singular idea of a single supreme being. As Sigmund Freud has suggested in his book *Moses and Monotheism* (1939), the idea most likely originated with the visionary Egyptian pharaoh Amenhotep IV (subsequently known, in one variation or another, as Akhenaton, Akhenaten, Akhnaton, or Ikhnaton) approximately 3,350 years ago. The exclusive worship of a single supreme being (namely, the Egyptian sun god, Aton) among the ancient Egyptians for a brief period most likely influenced the subsequent presence and consequent development of monotheism among, first, the Jews; then, the Zoro-astrians; next, the Christians; and finally, the Muslims.

It is an enduring tribute to that curious amalgam of human pride, hope and optimism that, with no exception since the dawn of monotheism, man, within the intellectual confines of the cultures of either Judaism, Zoroastrianism, Christianity, or Islam, has continually inferred his origin as deriving not from any things inferior, but from something superior, to himself.

The concept of this single supreme being—be it the Aton of the ancient Egyptians during the brief reign of Amenhotep IV; the Yahweh of the Jews; the Brahma (that dominating equilibratory spiritual force between Vishnu and Shiva) of the Hindus; the Ahura Mazda of the Zoroastrians; the God: Father, Son, and Holy Spirit of the Christians; the Allah of the Muslims; or the Sat Nam of the Sikhs—is essentially the same. It is the concept of a single dominating intelligence—an absolute and ultimate rational power—independent of, and the source of, all other things and beings. It is the concept of God, and inasmuch as everything that is is fully dependent upon it, it is nothing other than good. We will have much to say with respect to the symbolism of God further on in our discussion.

All of the various major forms of the concept of a single supreme being in religious thinking most likely emerged through a process of conceptual reductionism which culminated in the monism of Amenhotep (and, subsequently, of Moses), the dualism of Zoroaster (which, as we shall see, influenced considerably the further development of monotheism), and that curious amalgamation of monism and dualism that is so clearly discernible in the Hindu trinity of sovereign deities. Although Hinduism probably preceded Zoroastrianism by at least one thousand years, the dualism of Vishnu and Shiva does not present a dichotomy between good and evil quite like that found in the dualism of Ahura Mazda and Ahriman. For Hindus, Brahma is the symbol of the ultimate reality, while all of the opposites in the phenomena of worldly existence are reflected in the dual concept of Vishnu, the preserver, and Shiva, the destroyer. But Shiva per se is not necessarily evil. The god of destruction is also variously seen as the god of fertility, of regeneration, and of justice. While Vishnu is generally acknowledged as good, the goodness of Vishnu is a highly relative goodness, a goodness of a kind that makes things better, like the magnanimity of a hero, and not necessarily the kind of absolute goodness that ultimately leads to *moksha*. Accordingly, we are unable to conclude that the dualism of Vishnu and Shiva in Hinduism presents very much more than a murky dichotomy between good and evil.

On the other hand, the dualism of Ahura Mazda and Ahriman in Zoroastrianism projects a well-defined dichotomy, an image of worldly existence in which two opposing camps—the forces of good and the forces of evil—clash unrelentingly until the end of the 12,000-year history of the world, when the forces of the Wise Lord will decisively defeat those of the Evil Spirit. The commonalities of Zoroastrianism, Judaism, Christianity, and Islam—the concept of Satan; the concept of a universal *saoshyant*, or savior, for the spiritual well-being of human beings; and the concept of a powerful and benevolent entourage of angels and archangels in opposition to an evil entourage of demons and arch-fiends—strongly suggest the influence of Zoroastrianism in the development of the current three great world religions of monotheism. An initial influence on Judaism probably occurred at and after the time of the Babylonian Exile in the 6th century B.C.; a further influence on Judaism (as well as an initial influence on ancient Greek thought) probably occurred after the conquests of Alexander the Great in the 4th century B.C.; the influence on Christianity must have occurred by means of an intimate association with Judaism from the time of Christ along with a general exposure to Zoroastrian influences in Hellenistic culture; and the influence on Islam undoubtedly occurred just a few centuries later on the Arabian peninsula through a prolonged exposure to one or another of any of these influences.

We can conclude that the process of conceptual reductionism in religious thinking which occurred as a highly significant phase in the evolution of human thought over the past five or six thousand years culminated at once in a highly refined concept of a single supreme being—of a god at once powerful and good—and, of necessity, because of the unignorable empirical evidence of the presence and persistence of evil in the world, in the concept of a second sovereign deity—of a hostile spirit at once powerful and evil—presently and under certain circumstances coequal with and independent of, but ultimately (in all places where both deities should be present) unconditionally subordinate to, the original supreme being.

With the crystallization of the concepts of a good supernatural supreme being, a supreme being that is generally seen to be beneficial for human existence providing that an appropriate conciliatory relationship has been both established and maintained between this supreme being and human beings, and an antithetical counterpart, an evil sovereign spirit that is generally seen to be detrimental for human existence despite the best human efforts to reject such a being—that is, with the emergence, first, of the duality of Ahura Mazda and Ahriman in Zoroastrianism and, then, of God and the Devil in Judaism, Christianity, and Islam—came further imaginative speculation about an appropriate place and a permanent home for each of the two supernatural supreme beings, a place where either of them could dwell with kindred supernatural beings but also a place where either of them would hold absolute sovereignty, a place at once independent of, and removed from, the limits of time and of the natural universe. So emerged the related concepts of heaven and hell, of the kingdom of God and the kingdom of the Lord of Darkness.

With respect to the conception of the afterlife during the progress of the evolution of human thought, man most likely imagined at first that upon death, his animus, or spirit—that intangible and invisible portion of his being that had provided energy for, and movement of, his body over and above consciousness and thought in his mind—continued to live, either by occupying a fixed or a changing position in the earth, water, or air, or by inhabiting another being or object. Later, around the time of the appearance of the earliest civilizations, man began to conceive of a fixed and certain location of the home for the surviving spirits of the dead, but this location, albeit within the natural world, was not one which anyone could ever expect to discover during the course of his or her earthly existence. This home for the spirits of the dead was generally imagined to be located somewhere hidden far beneath the surface of the earth, in a place of unknown caverns and underground rivers—the *Arallû* of the Babylonians, the Sheol of the Hebrews, and the Hades of the Greeks. At about the same time, a time in the cultural evolution of mankind when the lives of most people were increasingly coming to be dominated, regulated, and imperiled by oligarchies of monarchs, nobles, and priests, most people almost certainly imagined that life after death would have little or no more freedom than life itself, and man most likely began to develop the concept of the judgment of souls after death, imagining both a place of permanent reward for the spirits of those who did not fail to observe the prevailing norms of their societies while they were alive, and a place of continuous punishment for the spirits of those who did. Accordingly, heaven came to be conceived of as the permanent home not only of God but of the spirits of all of those whose lives were good, a place of eternal happiness—Paradise—the Garden of Eden—while hell came to be conceived of as the permanent home not only of Satan but of the spirits of all of those whose lives were evil, a place of eternal alienation, pain, and misery—Tartarus—the Lake of Fire.With the ascendence of the law of reason over the law of nature within the evolution and history of the human species, an ascendence which is relatively recent and which we can date from approximately 1690, the evolution of religious thought has taken a new direction. We still retain concepts of heaven and hell, but the imports of the concepts are no longer the same as they once were. Today, heaven has become a symbol of the terminus in the evolution of reason, arising at the intersections of time and eternity, and of the universe and infinity, and defining a place of perfect and endless human existence. But if I should live a long and happy life, and die in my sleep without pain at a time when my body is frail and decaying, can I rationally expect—or do I need to hope for—something more? Our species, for all of its advancement beyond the other species of life on the earth and for all of its recent progress in the development of scientific technology, can only be seen, with neither inaccuracy nor dishonesty, as exceedingly primitive, when it has neither secured world peace nor laid down the foundation for a universal morality. We have all been born into a world in which interpersonal relationships remain adversarial and confrontational, in which illusion is popularly more tenable than truth, and in which the course of the lives of human beings, whether considered individually or collectively, are driven more readily by the interaction of natural urges, desires, and emotions than by a determined commitment to the exercise of reason. In a world in which human beings, even those who are equals among equals (as with the majority of the people in democratic nations), even yet commonly inflict injury upon one another, upon other forms of sentient life, and upon even the biosphere upon which all forms of life depend, we have unhappily given birth to a new and special meaning for the concept of hell. In the words of Jean-Paul Sartre, from his one-act play, *No Exit* (1944), "Hell is other people." It is this, and nothing else, and it will remain such until human beings willfully endeavor to transform human nature through the latent power of reason.

The concepts of God and heaven will endure for as long as human beings strive to attain perfection. But once we come to terms with the limitations of nature, that is, once we effect a thorough reconciliation between reason and nature, we can surely abandon our interest in heaven as a final destination for eternal life and retain only our interest in heaven as a place of perfect human existence, replacing the concept of a remote and unknowable place with the integrated concepts of an hospitable personal environment and a universal democratic society.

The concepts of hell and the evil supernatural supreme being will endure for as long as evil persists. But once we learn to predict and to control, to avoid, or to escape the disasters of nature, and once we learn to eliminate our own evil behavior, these concepts will continue to be present with us only in mythology. Is it not in our common best interest, for the sake of our permanent well-being, that we should now attempt to achieve these objectives in as little time as possible? Is not the emotion of happiness in human beings not an accident of nature but a combined physiological reaction and mental reflection that is essentially dependent upon a determined and unrelenting application of the rational faculties of the human mind? Are we not truly being irresponsible for ourselves and our posterity if we persist in evading these critical questions?

At this juncture in our discussion, we should call attention to the distinction between conventional and nonconventional symbolism, a distinction that is true of symbolism both in art and in religion. When the import of a symbol lies at the intersection of objectivity and subjectivity, which is to say, when the import of the symbol is clearly recognized by the majority of the members of a group as well as by any particular individual within the group, the symbol either is (or is able to become) a conventional symbol. A conventional symbol is one that is used by a group or a subgroup to convey a common and readily-recognized import. In religion, for example, common symbols that have long been used throughout a variety of cultures include light, lightning, and fire; the sun; the moon; certain stars (either planets of the solar system or distant suns) and star constellations; the sea; certain rivers, mountains, and mountain ranges; the tree (whether the tree in general, as the tree of life or the tree of the knowledge of good and evil, or a particular tree, as that variety of fig tree alternatively known as the *bo* tree or the pipal tree); soma, *haoma*, and related mushrooms, cacti, and shrubs that contain hallucinogens or stimulants; a multitude of particular animals, such as baboons, monkeys, elephants, bulls, cows, bison, horses, deer, antelope, rams, boars, tigers, lions, cats, bears, wolves, jackals, dogs, hawks, peacocks, ibises, vultures, giant turtles, snakes (especially the cobra), scorpions, and certain human beings; and imaginary animals (notably the dragon, the unicorn, and the feathered serpent, or Quetzalcoatl), the major body parts of which are fashioned in the mind's eye from the corresponding body parts of various real animals. The imports that are generally attached to each of these symbols include power or prowess and goodness or evil.

If a symbol is not or cannot be used by a group or a subgroup, it may be said to be a nonconventional symbol. These include symbols that convey imports that are unique to particular unrelated and unaffiliated individuals or that may be common among various individuals although they are not yet commonly used or even generally recognized by groups or subgroups. For example, a particular initiate in a puberty rite of a primitive society may be the only person to attach an import to some phenomenon that he (whether in the company of others or not) has experienced.

Whether symbols are conventional or nonconventional, they may at times be both at once. This is so in particular with respect to the symbolism of God and it is so because symbols can and do change their meanings over a long period of time as a direct effect of the evolution of human thought. We may call this change in the meaning of the symbol an import shift. I submit that an initial shift in the meaning of God, comprised of two alternative and almost mutually-exclusive forms, occurred approximately two thousand years ago and that a new, uniform, and final shift is now just beginning to occur.

The sovereign source of monism may be traced to the ancient Aryans of the Iranian plateau at least four thousand years ago. At that time, God, or the ultimate source of reality, was conceived of as a symbol for knowledge, truth, and wisdom—and the symbols of God included various phenomena that served as metaphors for knowledge, truth, and wisdom—to wit, the sun, light, lightning, and fire. Furthermore, it was thought that the optimal (and possibly the only) way to encounter or to approach such absolute truth was through an extraordinary and singular human experience, an experience independent of normal sensory perception and rational cognition—in short, a mystical experience of a kind most easily induced by procuring and ingesting certain chemical substances so as to create hallucinations and a heightened awareness of reality. The ancient Aryans who left the Iranian plateau at about 1800 B.C. to invade India and to establish the Hindu religion, and the Aryans who remained behind, eventually to establish the Zoroastrian religion, shared in common three cardinal aspects of their respective religions: (1) the conception and use of fire as a symbol of the ultimate reality; (2) the ritual of preparing and drinking an intoxicating and exhilarating beverage, or sacred liquor—the soma of the Brahmans and the *haoma* of the Zoroastrians; and (3) a dependence upon a body of sacred scriptures, each bearing striking similarities with the other with respect to form, content, and the very language in which it was written—the Veda of the Brahmans and the Avesta of the Zoroastrians.

After a course of about thirteen hundred years, Buddhism emerged from Hinduism in India and, about another five hundred years later (also in India), Mahayana Buddhism branched off from the original religion established by the Buddha (which continued as Theravada Buddhism). Mahayana Buddhism then gradually disseminated to Tibet, Mongolia, China, Korea, and Japan. The distinguishing feature of Buddhism, in contrast to Hinduism, was a stronger focus on ethics rather than metaphysics, and the distinguishing feature of Mahayana Buddhism, in contrast either to Hinduism or to Theravada Buddhism, was the vision of a path to nirvana (the Buddhist conception of the ultimate goal of human existence which supplanted the related Hindu conception of *moksha*) open to all people rather than only a privileged oligarchy or a dedicated elite. Although Buddhism initially rejected the conception of supernatural supreme beings (including even that of Brahma), Mahayana Buddhism eventually began to deify the Buddha, and the Mahayana conception of the ultimate reality, or Buddhahood, was presented as that of an absolutely benevolent and compassionate spiritual being. This gradual change in the meaning of the symbolism of God, from the Lord of Wisdom to the Lord of Compassion, may be called the great Eastern divine import shift.

While these events were taking place in central and eastern Asia, Zoroastrianism was emerging in ancient Persia, from which it came to exert a powerful influence, either directly or indirectly, upon the development and dissemination of each of the three great closely-related religions of monotheism. These religions, of course, originated in western Asia, gradually spread to Europe and most of Africa, and eventually reached North America and South America. The Hellenistic world in which Jesus lived and taught was an amalgam of the vestiges of ancient Mesopotamian, Egyptian, and Phoenician religious beliefs, of Judaism and Zoroastrianism, and of various ancient Greek philosophies, including such practical moral philosophies as Epicureanism and Stoicism. Like the contrast between Mahayana and Theravada, the distinguishing feature of Christianity (as it developed up to the time of the conversion of Constantine the Great in 312—shortly after which Christianity became the official religion of the Roman Empire), in contrast to the Judaism from which it emerged, was the vision of a path to salvation open to all people rather than only a minority comprised of a people chosen by God. Unlike the predominately ethical focus of Buddhism, the focus of Christianity (as it has continued to develop up to the present day) may generally be said to be centered equally upon both its metaphysics and its ethics. But like the concept of Buddhahood, as it ultimately emerged in Mahayana Buddhism, the concept of God in Christianity became that of an absolutely benevolent, caring, and compassionate supernatural supreme being, a God that remains all-powerful but that turns its own power against itself out of love for all of mankind. This new and transformed God of Christianity stands in conspicuous contrast to the original and wrathful God of Judaism. This abrupt change in the meaning of the symbolism of God—anticipated by the concept of the messiah which appeared first in Zoroastrianism, then in Judaism, and finally in Christianity—from the exacting creator of mankind to the loving redeemer of mankind, may be called the great Western divine import shift. As we have said, it is but one of the two alternative and almost mutually-exclusive forms and manifestations of an initial shift in the original meaning of the symbolism of God, each form and manifestation occurring at about the same time approximately two thousand years ago but in different and widely-separated regions of the world.

We have also suggested that a new, uniform, and final shift is now just beginning to occur. As the original meaning of the symbolism of God arose in the Iranian plateau among the ancient Aryans, and as the initial shift from the original meaning of the symbolism of God emerged (or erupted), developed, and disseminated in opposite directions along a horizontal axis from ancient Persia, so is it almost as certain that the new, uniform, and final shift from the eastern and western versions of the initial divine import shift will not only be simultaneous but ubiquitous. Accordingly, it may aptly be referred to as the great Universal divine import shift.

I will present the nature of this import shift, as I see it, a little later on in the present discourse. At the same time, I will discuss the major ramification of this import shift as it should appear most likely to affect the future of theism in religion. At this juncture, however, let us digress briefly to explore the meanings of the major conventional symbols of Buddhism and Christianity: the *dharmachakra* and the cross. We will begin with the *dharmachakra*.

Buddhism has created or adopted a number of symbols to convey such intents as truth, purity, tranquility, protection from evil, freedom from suffering, the essential teachings of the Buddha, and the most significant places and events in the life of the Buddha. The symbols may be things, either living or nonliving, or representations of such things, or combinations of things, such as may be found in flags, banners, and insignias; in painting, sculpture, and architecture; and even in certain positions and gestures of the adjoined left and right hands. To provide a pair of examples, the *bo* tree is a symbol of enlightenment because, according to legend, the Buddha received enlightenment while seated beneath a *bo* tree, while the deer (or a pair of deer) is a symbol of the teachings of the Buddha because the Buddha preached his first sermon in a deer park at Sarnath (an ancient religious center located approximately four or five miles north of modern Varanasi—formerly known as Benares—the great holy city of the Hindus situated on the Ganges River in Uttar Pradesh, India).

One group of symbols represents truth in sensory perception. Hence, Buddhists use the mirror as a symbol for acuity in seeing; the lute, in hearing; the incense burner, in smelling; fruit, in tasting; and silk, in touching.

The *dharmachakra* is one of another group of symbols, commonly known as the Eight Auspicious Symbols, which also includes the lotus flower, the right-coiled white conch, the parasol or umbrella, the victory banner, the golden fish, the auspicious knot, and the vase of treasure. The *dharmachakra* is the wheel (*chakra*) of the law (dharma) and it is the principal symbol of the ethical teachings of Siddhartha Gautama. It is generally depicted as a wheel with eight spokes which, of course, signify the eight moral tenets comprising the Eightfold Path, the fourth of the Four Noble Truths. Let us consider each of the two parts of the symbol: first, the dharma itself—the core of Buddhist ethics as presented in the Eightfold Path—and then the threefold significance of the wheel.

Briefly stated, the Four Noble Truths are as follows: (1) every form and entity of existence experiences constant and unavoidable suffering and is a part of an inescapable and unending cycle of existence; (2) desire is the cause of all suffering; (3) desire can be arrested, diminished, and, ultimately, eliminated; (4) the acceptance and practice of the moral conduct prescribed by the Eightfold Path will vanquish desire and bring a permanent end to an existence of suffering. The eight moral tenets of the Eightfold Path fall within three broad categories of human moral thought and behavior: self-discipline, moral knowledge, and moral action. Self-discipline, or mental discipline, includes right effort (or right endeavor), right mindfulness (that is, being sufficiently aware and adequately informed), and right concentration. Right concentration is necessary to free the mind from its attraction to immediate and temporary appearances as well as its attachment to customary but illusory values. Right concentration almost always requires disciplined practice, such as is usually achieved by learning certain techniques and performing various exercises of the traditional Hindu practice of yoga. Moral knowledge, or wisdom, entails attaining and maintaining right views, and having and fulfilling good intentions. Moral action, or ethical behavior, includes right speech, right conduct, and right livelihood. Right speech requires refraining from lies, slander, disparaging or inflammatory remarks, and idle or detrimental gossip. Right conduct prohibits killing, stealing, and unchastity. Right livelihood prohibits earning one's living, whether directly or indirectly, through any of a variety of useless or abusive activities, such as by killing, making weapons, divination, telling fortunes, and dealing in dangerous and harmful substances.

A Buddhist's acceptance of the underlying rationale for the Eightfold Path is the culmination of Buddhist thought and practice. To follow the Eightfold Path is to embrace the absolute truth, to adhere to the universal law of existence, to engage in the practice of dharma—the only means by which human beings can overcome natural desire and attain lasting peace, tranquility, and purity of existence.

It is highly significant that the dharma is enclosed within the hub and the rim of the wheel in the *dharmachakra*. Quite obviously, the wheel, as one of the most basic tools of rudimentary technology, is something extremely useful for human beings. The wheel, then, is a symbol of utility. Furthermore, as a unique tool with a specific function, that of enabling a person to move, either to move himself or herself or to move his or her personal property, the wheel is a thing that enables a person to change—not only to change from one location to another but from one condition to another. The wheel, then, is also at once a symbol of transportation and of transformation. Finally, the wheel appears as a symbol both in Hinduism and in Buddhism. The Hindu wheel is a symbol of samsara, of the endless cycle of birth, death, and rebirth; hence, it is a symbol of cosmic destiny. In Buddhism, on the other hand, an abrupt shift in the import of the Hindu wheel occurs. The Hindu wheel is supplanted by the wheel of the law, which becomes a symbol of the path to nirvana, of the ultimate release from samsara, of the sole means to the permanent end of suffering. The *dharmachakra*, then, is not only a symbol of utility and a symbol of change but a symbol of nirvana, or existential extinguishment, of liberation, of freedom, of ultimate happiness, of the ultimate goal of human existence.

With the emergence of Mahayana Buddhism, we can detect a gradual slight shift in the import of the *dharmachakra*. Since Mahayana conceives of the Buddha as both the incarnation of the universal law of existence and a being above and beyond the constraints of the same law, the Buddha becomes an external being, the only being that attains nirvana without existential extinguishment (which is to say, in the language of Buddhism, that the Mahayana Buddha attains nirvana with a perpetual remainder). As likely as not, the deification of the Buddha was an equation of the Buddha with the Hindu Brahma—the supernatural supreme being or absolute truth and the incarnation or ultimate source of universal law. The Buddha is then able to return to the world in one form or another on various occasions to assist human beings to see the truth, to follow the Eightfold Path, and to attain nirvana. Likewise, the various bodhisattvas were generally seen often to postpone their attainment of nirvana, and sometimes even to sacrifice themselves to a very great degree by transferring to others in need much of the merit deriving and accruing from their own past good karma so as to assist other sentient beings to attain enlightenment. Accordingly, two new virtues arise in addition to those enumerated in the Eightfold Path: the supreme virtues of universal compassion and sacrificial love. Hence, the import of the *dharmachakra* expands as the *dharmachakra* gradually becomes not only a symbol of the Eightfold Path but of universal compassion and sacrificial love. With this slight shift, the import of the *dharmachakra* begins to manifest a close affinity with that that ultimately comes to be attached to the symbol of the Christian cross.

Like Buddhism, Christianity has created or adopted a number of symbols to convey certain intents. These may be classified as falling under either of two categories: (1) those representing the Godhead and (2) those representing the divine sacrifice in behalf of mankind.

The symbol for God the Father is curiously inconspicuous in Christianity. Undoubtedly, the concept of an ultimate reality that is at once within and without the limits of time and space defies symbolic representation. Perhaps the best attempt to create some kind of representation occurred when Michelangelo completed his mural painting *The Creation of Adam* on the ceiling of the Sistine Chapel between 1508 and 1512. In this fresco, God is depicted as a powerful mature man, not unlike the earlier portrayals of Zeus and Jupiter in the visual arts of ancient Greece and Rome.

The symbol for God the Son is seen more frequently. Generally, it is incorporated into the symbols representing the divine sacrifice but where it is presented independently, it is most often seen in the image of a fish because the letters of the Greek alphabet which spell the Greek word for fish, *ichthos*, form an acronym for Jesus Christ Son of God Savior.

The symbol for God the Holy Spirit is generally depicted as a dove because the accounts of the baptism of Jesus in the gospels describe the descent of the Spirit of God in the likeness of a dove that lights upon the person of Jesus.

Christian symbols that commonly depict the divine sacrifice include the lamb (representing the sacrificial victim), bread and wine (representing the flesh and blood of the sacrificial victim), and the cross (representing the instrument of the sacrifice). Of these, the cross is, of course, the most widely-used symbol in Christianity.

The origin of the divine sacrifice can be traced back to the animal and human sacrifices of primitive religion. By the time of the onset of Judaism, human thought and sensibility had so progressed that human sacrifice had widely become repugnant. Hence, in the account of the trial of Abraham's faith in Genesis, Chapter 22, God compassionately provides an animal for sacrifice (the "ram caught in a thicket by his horns") to serve as an acceptable substitute for a human victim (Isaac, Abraham's son) after God becomes assured of Abraham's absolute devotion.

The early history of Judaism is an enactment of the story of the reciprocity, or covenant, between God and the chosen people. The story is very familiar: God chooses a certain person (Abraham) and all of this person's progeny (the Jewish people) and offers to provide for all of their needs—in other words, to guarantee their happiness—in exchange for their absolute and permanent devotion to God. Once a certain critical event in the history of these people should occur, their devotion to God will henceforth be clearly manifested to all of mankind through their steadfast adherence to the divine law, or the Torah (the essence of which is expressed in the Decalogue, or the Ten Commandments), as it eventually comes to be revealed to them by God. But both before and after the Torah has been given to them, the chosen people continually fall short of fulfilling the requirements of their side of the agreement, and God continually punishes them both by withholding divine favor and by permitting natural disasters and human enemies to harm them, until eventually they come to repent and the covenant consequently becomes restored. In time, the Jewish people began to anticipate the coming of a messiah, whose assistance, leadership, and mediation would enable them to effect a permanent covenantal reconciliation. Now, Christianity is predicated on the long history of the chosen people, just as is Judaism, but the position of Christianity with respect to the ultimate consequence of that long history is radically different from that of Judaism. As interpreted by Christianity, the bittersweet cycle of sin and repentance recurs throughout the long history of the chosen people until, ultimately, God comes to break the endless and hopeless cycle by engaging in an act of self-sacrifice not only in behalf of the chosen people but in behalf of all of the other people of the world. This act, of course, occurs with the crucifixion, death, and resurrection of Jesus, the Son of God, the Savior of mankind. The cross, then, becomes at once the symbol of the divine sacrifice and the symbol of the new covenant between God and mankind, a covenant in which no person need ever again fear to suffer the consequences of failing to fulfill the requirements of his or her side of the agreement, inasmuch as the remedy for his or her inevitable breach of the agreement has already been provided and effected by God. Furthermore, each person's requirements under the new covenant become radically simple: all that is required of one is that he or she manifests his or her absolute and permanent devotion to

God both by loving God and by loving all people with neither condition nor exception.

There are striking similarities between the ethical conduct prescribed by the Ten Commandments as summarized in the great commandment of Jesus and the ethical conduct prescribed by the Eightfold Path. There is also a striking similarity between the universal compassion and sacrificial love of the Buddha or of the various bodhisattvas of Mahayana Buddhism and the universal compassion and sacrificial love of the God of Christianity. We have already mentioned that, together, the Christian God and the Mahayana Buddha indicate a shift in the original divine import—a shift from the God of omnipotence and omniscience to the God of compassion and redemption. We have also suggested that another divine import shift is at hand, one that is universal, and one that will be permanent—a shift from the God of compassion and redemption to something new and entirely different. To understand the nature of this divine import shift, we must now attempt to reveal the symbolism of God as it is present to the human mind in the modern world. The ensuing discussion can serve as a means to this end.

What is it that a person means when he or she talks of God today? We will attempt to answer this question as accurately as we can. We will begin by asserting that the word "God" is a symbol of something, just as the word "chair" is a symbol of something. The word "chair" is a symbol of a piece of furniture intended to be sat in and typically having four vertical legs supporting a horizontal seat and a vertical back for one person. But the word "God" is far more difficult to define because very few persons (if anyone at all) have (has) ever perceived God. Accordingly, the word "God" most likely remains a symbol of a concept formed over a very long period of time in the human imagination. We are now prepared to examine the general quality and attributes of this concept.

God is a symbol of a blissful supreme being, a supreme being that is blissful either because it is not subject to the requirements of the law of nature (meaning that this being has no need to eat or to drink, to eliminate waste, to grow or to heal, to reproduce, and to fear the predation, aggression, or competition of other beings) or because it is perfect (meaning that this being is master of everything, and is deficient in nothing, that will enable it to satisfy all of the requirements of the law of nature). If the former alternative were to be true, we possess no understanding of it since a being that is not subject to the requirements of the law of nature either is subject to the requirements of a nature of some other universe that is so alien to us as to be fully incomprehensible or is altogether above and beyond nature. In either condition, we neither possess nor can ever attain an understanding of such a being since our knowledge derives from our experiences within our own natural environment. Accordingly, our concept of such a being resides wholly in our imaginations, which have given birth to the concept, and not in our reason. If the latter alternative were to be true, wherein we conceive of a blissful supreme being that is blissful because it is master of all that is necessary to satisfy the requirements of its existence, still we possess no understanding of it since, with the possible exception of a minute number of witnesses throughout history whose testimonies most likely have arisen as the consequence of a fantasy, an illusion, or an hallucination, we have acquired no direct evidence of such a being within the confines of our natural environment. Accordingly, our concept of such a being likewise resides wholly in our imaginations and not in our reason.

God is a symbol of all that remains either, on the one hand, unknown but not unknowable or, on the other hand, unknown and forever unknowable to the human mind. Now, to be sure, that which is unknowable would appear to have no relevance for human affairs or for the continuous quest to attain (or to recover) and then to maintain (or to secure) human happiness. On the other hand, both reason and knowledge are instrumental for the satisfactory conduct of human affairs and the successful pursuit of human happiness. In the course of learning, it would appear that as knowledge should grow, the unknown should shrink. Actually, and paradoxically, both knowledge and the unknown grow together. This is so because as our knowledge grows, so grows also our awareness of the magnitude of that which we do not know. Indeed, most scholars are relatively ignorant of advanced knowledge within disciplines outside of their respective fields of expertise. Accordingly, insofar as God is a symbol of all that remains unknown but not unknowable, the concept of God should remain coterminous with the length of the survival of the human species plus the lengths of the survival of all potential natural species which may, at some point in the distant future, be able to trace their descent directly (or perhaps even indirectly) to Homo sapiens. For rational beings, then, beings which posit hypotheses that must always be accompanied with grounds for a reasonable expectation that the validity of such will admit, with some degree of probability (however slight or remote), to eventual confirmation, God is a symbol of existential perfection and of all that is perfectible in human beings. This is the object of the great Universal divine import shift.

At this juncture in our discourse, I would like to introduce a similitude between the concept of God as it has been construed from the time of the universal divine import shift and the concept of the ultimate synthesis of the two fundamental modalities of being as it has been presented by Sartre in his magnum opus of existential philosophy, *Being and Nothingness* (1943). In the former abstraction, we must say that God has become no more than a symbol of existential perfection and human perfectibility. In the latter, Sartre posits the ultimate reality of being-in-itself-for-itself and, in Part Four, Chapter Two, Section I, he acknowledges that "It is this ideal which can be called God." However, the union of being-in-itself—being that is what it is—and being-for-itself—being that is what it is not and that is not what it is—is contradictory and, consequently, impossible. It is certainly obvious that Sartre is suggesting that the concept of God is no more than a futile invention of the human imagination, an endless longing, an ignis fatuus. In his own words, from Section I of the conclusion of the book, he states:

we must establish that the real is an abortive effort to attain to the dignity of the self-cause. Everything happens as if the world, man, and man-in-the-world succeeded in realizing only a missing God. Everything happens therefore as if the in-itself and the for-itself were presented in a state of disintegration in relation to an ideal synthesis. Not that the integration has ever *taken place* but on the contrary precisely because it is always indicated and always impossible.

Now, perfection implies a changeless state whereas human beings, like all life-forms, continually evolve, ever adapting to long-term changes in the natural environment. Therefore, human perfection remains an anomalous and impossible goal: all efforts to sustain it over the long run must inevitably fail; furthermore, perfection implies an absolute state whereas human existence, like all existence, is always conditional. Consequently, we will do better if we were to come to accept that optimality, and not perfection, is the most realistic and appropriate end of all human conduct. In light of this conclusion, we will presently advance the argument that the human species will do best to abandon altogether the concept of God—once the species comes to agree to favor, to encourage, and to expect the habitual and customary use of reason over imagination, and once it is able to supplant an archaic and obsolete faith in the supernatural with the happy combination of a confident new self-reliance (by which we must mean the self-reliance of the entire species taken as a whole as well as of each person in the world) and a universal respect for all sentient beings without exception or condition. These critical changes in human thought and behavior will require the highest degree of honesty among human beings, that we all learn to be as honest with ourselves as we are with all other people, that we refrain from inauthentic and unjust personal behavior or, in the words of Sartre, that we do not act in bad faith. The dependence of reason upon truth has been clearly recognized since the rise of ancient Greek philosophy, as has the apparent affinity between truth, goodness, and beauty. Now, I have considered at length the particular nature of goodness in all of my previous books but it is the exclusive province of the present work to consider the particular nature of truth and of beauty. It will serve our purpose at this time to consider the former in order to lay a foundation for the advancement of an argument that the concept of a supernatural supreme being, or of an ultimate reality beyond the limits of space and time—that the presence of belief in the absence of reason—that the practice of religion—create more injury than benefit for mankind and, as a consequence, that all of these concepts, beliefs, and practices—as a directly-imminent and ever-increasing threat to human well-being and cultural progress—ought to be rejected and abandoned as early in our common future as possible.

We may begin by asking the question, "What is truth?" It seems to us that the most succinct expression of the definition of truth can only be, "Truth is objectivity." If then we should ask, "What is objectivity?," we can reply, "Objectivity is that cognitive condition that operates on objects, phenomena, or conditions in the realm of sensible experience that are perceptible by all observers and insusceptible to individual misinterpretation." With truth so defined, we can proceed to identify its three fundamental categories: representational fidelity, empirical evidence, and subjective authenticity. Let us now examine them, one by one.

Representational fidelity is concerned with the truthfulness of the symbols commonly used in interpersonal communication, whether such symbols are mere words and ideograms or the symbolism of religion, art, and the other major categories of human concern and activity, and with establishing criteria that can be commonly accepted, widely used, and highly efficacious in determining the truthfulness of the meaning of all that may be conveyed through the symbols, from the most simple and basic of conveyances (the microsymbolism) to the most complex and expansive of messages (the macrosymbolism). For example, a good dictionary is invaluable for establishing and maintaining objectivity with respect to the meaning that is conveyed through one's choice of words in communication. Here, we must acknowledge that our objectivity is not absolute but relative, not perfect but optimal. A universal language, if one were to exist, would provide our words with an objectivity that would most closely approach perfection. In the absence of an acceptable and practicable universal language, the English language is perhaps the next best language to provide our words with the optimal degree of objectivity, inasmuch as it is a language spoken by a large number of people dispersed throughout a considerable portion of the world and it is also a very rich language—functioning as the product of an amalgam of two fundamental Indo-European languages (West Germanic, through Old English, and Latin, primarily through French) with an extraordinary abundance of loanwords from many other languages. The vocabulary of Modern English presently contains more than a million words and it is generally considered to be the largest vocabulary of any of the languages of the world.

Wherever words must be translated from one language into another, some degree of a risk of misinterpretation arises. For example, Diné bizaad, the language of the Navajo Indians, possesses only one word for either of those colors which in English are designated by the words "blue" and "green." Accordingly, that which is really "blue" may be misinterpreted as "green" and, conversely, that which is really "green," as "blue." (The word in Diné bizaad for "blue" or for "green" is unquestionably accurate for "turquoise," a variable color which, on average, is apparent as a light greenish blue and which takes its name from the mineral of the same color that is indigenous to the American Southwest, where the Navajo have lived for centuries. For the Navajo, the color of the sky, of turquoise, and of cactus are virtually identical and they invented but one word for their designation. Had the Navajo not lived in the desert but in a land with luxuriant vegetation, they would have almost certainly invented two separate words for "green" and "blue.")

Similar problems can sometimes arise with the use of other conventional symbols. For example, the symbol of the Red Cross has been appropriate and effective in nations where Christianity is the major religion or where the influence of Christianity is not resisted but it was required to be recast as the Red

Crescent in almost all of the Islamic countries because the cross, as a symbol of Christianity, is deeply offensive to Muslims.

With respect to macrosymbolism, the intent of the philosophy of utilitarianism has been effectively conveyed through such writings as Bentham's *The Principles of Morals and Legislation* and Mill's *Utilitarianism*, while the accurate representation of the redemptive transformation of a certain pattern of human behavior from that of selfish greed to that of selfless heroism has been effectively conveyed through works of art, such as George Eliot's novel *Silas Marner* or Wagner's cycle of music dramas *The Ring of the Nibelung*.

Wherever the use of words and/or other conventional symbols succeeds in conveying their intended meanings, wherever thinkers succeed in communicating the essence of their thought without misunderstanding, and wherever artists succeed both in transmitting to others some impression of the concepts which underlie the creative intuitive insight and in arousing among others the emotions that are typically generated through a growing awareness and reinforced recognition of such concepts, we can say that the symbols and/or symbolisms are truthful, that they convey their intended intent, and that they possess representational fidelity.

Whenever we perceive an object in our natural environment, we are perceiving something that others perceive as well—since, with the exception of a relatively small subpopulation of persons suffering from perceptual defects, all human beings possess the same modalities of perception—and we refer to the object which we perceive by use of the name that others have already assigned to it. The perception of an object by any person who possesses the normal faculties of perception provides empirical evidence that the idea of the object is true. The flow of information proceeds from the object to the idea of the object. (This flow, of course, generally defines empiricism.) Now, let us proceed in the opposite direction. If we have an idea of something without possessing empirical evidence for it, our idea is either false or, at best, tentative, but not true, because we have not as yet uncovered any empirical evidence for it. If we can reasonably expect, even with the smallest degree of probability, that some empirical evidence in support of the truth of our idea may come to light in the future, our idea may continue as a hypothesis. Otherwise, our idea is false and, as such, we must reject it, with the sole exception that—as a product of our imagination, as an acknowledged fantasy, as an intriguing object of make-believe—it may have some measure of artistic, educational, or entertainment value.

Locke discusses in great detail both representational fidelity and empirical evidence in *An Essay Concerning Human Understanding*, although he refers to these categories of truth by different names (as "verbal truth" and "real truth"). Until the emergence of certain representatives of two distinct schools among the various critics and revisers of empiricist thought—of certain romanticists and existentialists—in the two centuries that followed the Enlightenment, there were very few who were neither fully nor largely ignorant of the third category of truth, that of subjective authenticity.

Among the most influential and noteworthy romanticists, we must mention: Blake, Thoreau, Rousseau, and Dostoyevsky; among the existentialists: Kierkegaard, Nietzsche, Heidegger, and Sartre.

The romanticists and existentialists recognized that, even in a world of reason and objectivity, human happiness remains essentially subjective and is largely self-determined. The general sense of their conclusions might be stated as follows. Each person is autonomous. One person cannot fully know how another person thinks or feels. One person cannot create complete happiness for another person. On the whole, one must freely attempt to create one's own happiness. This kind of effort requires personal conduct in tandem with a new inwardly-directed dimension of honesty.

In *Being and Nothingness*, Sartre is explicit in his description of this kind of honesty. He contrasts it with its all-too-prevalent opposite, "bad faith," which he describes as "not believing what one believes" (by which he means that a person retains doubts about, is not fully convinced of, is not thoroughly committed to, the things that he or she professes to believe). In Part One, Chapter Two, Section III, he states:

> it is very true that bad faith does not succeed in believing what it wishes to believe. But it is precisely as the acceptance of not believing what it believes that it is bad faith. Good faith wishes to flee the "not-believing-what-one-believes" by finding refuge in being. Bad faith flees being by taking refuge in "not-believing-what-one-believes."

The conclusion, of course, is that subjective authenticity (and, by inference, personal happiness) is predicated upon a presence of absolute honesty or, stated conversely and perhaps a little more precisely, an absence of self-deception. Upon this foundation, the truth of subjective authenticity is then able to arise in a union of the processes of self-awareness, self-definition, and self-realization.

We will do well to observe that subjective inauthenticity is not quite the same as hypocrisy. In hypocrisy, one pretends to believe what one does not, or not to believe what one does, in order to deceive others. In subjective inauthenticity, to deceive oneself. One permits oneself to do so so as to relieve the anxiety that one always feels upon the onset of an awareness of one's unique selfhood and aloneness in the world. During the period of adolescence or in the earliest stage of adulthood, with the sincerity of innocence, a person more likely than not truly believes. But as time passes and the rational incongruities of what the person believes should increasingly happen to come to light in his or her own mind, the person will begin to believe what he or she does not, or not to believe what he or she does, and his or her equanimity gradually deteriorates as the person's disposition regresses back to the original state of anxiety. By this time, the person will have become aware of his or her self-deception and he or she will be living in bad faith.

It is apparent that one does not freely choose to enter into bad faith head-on but rather one slowly slips into it. It is never an immediate problem that is clearly recognizable from the start but a problem that increasingly comes to light over time. We can conclude, then, that bad faith finds its origin in disillusionment.

In short, a person will engage in self-deception only in order to *feel* good, and once the person recognizes that the feeling so achieved does not endure, he or she is able to abandon bad faith, to reject conventional beliefs, to cast off conventional roles, and to begin to pursue a course that will reveal the true meaning of his or her unique being and so secure genuine permanent personal happiness.

We will also do well to observe that our use of the term "subjective authenticity" should not be construed to imply that truth within this category of truth is not objective; on the contrary, by its use we mean only to imply that the origin of this kind of truth, unlike the origins of representational fidelity and empirical evidence, is wholly subjective. Each person will attain subjective authenticity in his or her own way, and the way that one person attains it may be entirely different from that of another. One cannot begin to experience full personal happiness until one begins to engage in a process of self-realization, but then the effect of subjective authenticity becomes totally objective: everyone in contact with the self-fulfilling person gradually becomes aware (by means of observing the appearance and the habitual conduct and demeanor of the self-fulfilling person) that that person has attained an obvious unchanging singular and unassailable happiness.

Having completed our discussion of the particular nature of truth (wherein we have effected a kind of marriage between empiricism and existentialism), we are now adequately prepared to evaluate the argument for atheism.

Let us begin by recapitulating the long history of theism and monism. At first, man almost certainly created through the power of his imagination a world of supernatural beings as compensation for the enormous inadequacies of personal ability and interpersonal cooperation in his ongoing effort to satisfy the needs and to avert the hurts of life. With the advent of civilization, man developed a compartmentalization and hierarchy of supernatural beings and he invented gods and goddesses, often including a dominant god and goddess, to preside over the natural and supernatural worlds. Next, someone somewhere in the world to the west of ancient Persia (from whence originated and disseminated the concept of either a duality or trinity of supreme beings), most probably Amenhotep IV of the 18th dynasty of ancient Egypt, conceived of a single supreme being; sometime a little later in India, someone (we cannot be certain who) derived the concept of an absolute ultimate reality, Brahman, out of Brahma, the sovereign god of the Hindu trinity of supreme gods. Thus arose the original divine import. After the passing of several more centuries and at a time approximately two thousand years ago, a radical shift took place with respect to the original meaning of the divine, from a conditionally benevolent (if not a totally indifferent) creator to an unconditionally benevolent redeemer. Throughout the transition from ancient history to modern history, the compassionate behavior of the divine redeemer (as recounted in the sacred writings of Christianity and Mahayana Buddhism) served as the supreme ethical model, and with the ascendence of empiricism throughout the West and those other parts of the world most deeply influenced by Western values, a second shift began to take place with respect to the common meaning of the great Eastern divine import shift and the great Western divine import shift, from an unconditionally benevolent redeemer to an ideal of existential perfection. Now, among the more than six billion people in the world today, there are a small number who still believe in animism of one form or another, others (as many of the members of the lower socio-economic classes in India) who still adhere to polytheism, many others who adhere to monotheism or monism and whose notion of the meaning of God or of an absolute ultimate reality either conforms with the original divine import or with the Eastern or Western version of the initial divine import shift, and still others who are subject in varying degrees to the cultural influence of either monotheism (in one form or another) or monism although they adhere to neither, who are highly doubtful that God may exist or that there may be an absolute ultimate reality, and whose notion of the meaning of God or of an absolute ultimate reality, influenced by the suppositional model of an unconditionally benevolent divine redeemer as presented in the form of a perfect human being, conforms with the ideal of human perfectibility. The unhappy consequences of this sociological phenomenon are not as immediately obvious as those flowing from differentials in the rates of technological progress among the various cultures but they involve the creation and fostering of misunderstanding, mistrust, and either tacit indifference or explicit ill will between one religious tradition or community and others that are different. If it were not for this enormous and dangerous disparity in the rate of the progress of the religious sensibility among the members of the human species, we could almost certainly conclude that religion is harmless and that we could allow it to persist without question for as long as it should appear to provide a measure of solace, comfort, and encouragement for at least some small portion of the general population.

We have said that from the time of his origin, man almost certainly invented the world of the supernatural and we have suggested that he did so for emotional reasons—to create hope in meeting the demands of survival by attempting to secure the assistance of existential powers beyond the limits of his own and to eliminate or to diminish anxiety and despair by attributing his failures and inadequacies to the malevolence of supernatural beings. We would now also suggest that, from the time that man first became aware of himself as an individual within a totality of like beings, he began to desire that his kind should have an apparent origin and, to attain that end, he invented a supernatural father for his protoprogenitor. Thus, the human species in its infancy created an imaginary father to settle the question of its apparent orphanhood. However, we must recognize that once a child grows up, whether such an individual has been an orphan or not, he or she no longer remains in need of a mother or a father—and so it is with the human species as a whole once the species comes of age, becomes culturally integrated, and achieves self-sufficiency.

We will now lay out the various reasons why the persistence of the concept of God, or of an ultimate reality that transcends time and space—why the persistence of faith in the supernatural—why the persistence of the practice of religion—create far more evil than good—and if our argument possesses sufficient merit, we will be unable not to conclude that these concepts, beliefs, and practices ought not to be permitted to continue but ought to be immediately rejected and quickly abandoned. Our argument is in three parts.

To begin, we must concede that religion has generally been ineffective in preventing war and that, in certain instances, it has actually functioned as the fundamental cause of war. This has happened in such instances because religious people came to regard the conduct of war as an exercise of divine power while they also came to regard as almost certainly beyond question and totally exempt from judgment the desire, will, and action of the deity who was seen to have initiated and directed such conduct. This attitude is not unlike that of those people who do not judge the pneumococcus bacterium because it is simply fulfilling its natural function of infecting various mammals, but that such people do not judge the pneumococcus bacterium does not prevent those same people from attempting to destroy the bacterium in an effort to prevent it from causing human deaths through pneumonia. In this light, we would do best not to consider the detrimental effects of the beliefs, practices, and influences of religion too naively.

Let us briefly examine a singular nexus between each of the three great religions of monotheism and war.

The sacred writings of Judaism state that God enabled the Jewish people to settle Palestine by directing them to make war against the native Canaanites. Is it not an offense against reason to be expected to believe that the God who formulated and transmitted the Ten Commandments is the same God who roused and directed the members of one society of human beings to rob and to murder the members of another?

The history of Islam records that Mohammed founded the Muslim community at Medina, where he and his followers seized the homes and wealth of all of the Jews who refused to convert to his new religion. Is it not an offense against reason to be expected to believe that the God who initiated and established a permanent covenant with the Jewish people is the same God who permitted and encouraged Mohammed to rob and to expel the Jews of Medina?

European history relates the conquest of Jerusalem by Christian knights during the First Crusade, where 10,000 Muslim and Jewish inhabitants of the city were brutally massacred. Is it not an offense against reason to be expected to believe that the God of the Jews and of the Muslims is the same God who inspired Pope Urban II to direct an appeal to all of Christendom to launch the Crusades?

The correct answer, the same for all three questions, depends upon whether or not the existence of God is independent of the existence of man. If so, the answer is yes. If not, the answer is no, since the concept of God arises solely in the imaginations of various people in different places at different times.

We can draw two inescapable inferences from the foregoing observations: one, that God does not exist (for which we will increasingly become ever more grateful than regretful) and two, that the practice of religion erects an absolute barrier to world peace.

Next, we can further infer that the practice of religion, except possibly for that of a singular universal religion, precludes all efforts to achieve peaceful world unification or to establish and to maintain effective universal morals and legislation. Religion often appears to promote worthy social objectives but its fundamental appeal resides in its enduring promise of providing an ultimate and inevitable personal advantage for each of its adherents. Hence, religion is essentially subjective and not objective. It attempts to approach ethical objectivity through metaphysical subjectivity, but by doing so, it increasingly undermines and ultimately betrays all objectivity.

Some religions are either totally or largely unconcerned with political organization. Others hold that political organization must only have divine direction in order to provide worthy and lasting meaningfulness for human affairs—either through direct and universal divine revelation (such that everyone everywhere can recognize the will of God) or through indirect and local divine revelation (as through specific persons believed to be divinely chosen to serve as representatives of God, which is to say, through prophets and/or prophetesses). But in the obvious absence of the former kind of divine revelation, rational people can only remain highly skeptical of the assertions of the claimants of the latter. In either event, man could not be the initiator but only the agent of political activity.

Progressive human well-being, universal personal freedom, universal human rights, universal social justice, and lasting world peace require a unified world. The moral foundation of a unified world must be rational. Religion is in all aspects, in all of its forms, and at all times, irrational; and it is in many respects, in some of its forms, and at certain times, antirational. Hence, religion and its practice can nowhere be relied upon to provide effective support for an emerging universal democratic initiative to achieve world political unification.

Finally, we can infer that the practice of religion precludes all efforts to remove and to prevent bad faith as the primary impediment to the attainment and perpetuation of human happiness. This is the most serious of the charges we must raise against religion since the prevalence of bad faith in religion not only encumbers each person's pursuit of happiness but almost certainly accounts for the powerlessness of religion to deal usefully, beneficially, and effectively with the two problems that we have already discussed.

With the words of Sartre, we have described bad faith as "not believing what one believes." Unlike hypocrisy, which is an intentional effort to deceive others and for which it is most often mistaken, bad faith is an intentional effort not to abandon a belief once one becomes aware that one no longer believes it. Bad faith is generally grounded in an atmosphere of uncertainty, ambivalence, and irresolution. The moral consequence of bad faith is evil in all of its forms— ignorance, apathy, and ineptitude—while the inevitable consequences of evil are all too well-known—pain, suffering, and misery. Accordingly, the early recognition and prompt elimination of bad faith is singularly instrumental for any discovery of, and access to, the various sources of human happiness.

We must now proceed to consider the effect of the presence of bad faith in each of the major categories of human concern and activity, beginning with those of society—economics, politics, and religion—and ending with those of each person—work and interpersonal relationships. Inasmuch as economics fully depends upon politics, our discussion of the latter should be sufficient to preclude any discussion of the former.

Diversity in politics is expressed along a continuum between freedom and justice. The one value expresses the personal moral ideal; the other, the social. The fulfillment of both values is necessary for general human happiness notwithstanding that the fulfillment of either one cannot be accomplished without the substantial sacrifice of the other. Hence, an equilibrium between freedom and justice is the most that we can expect, and such an equilibrium is best provided through democracy. Under a democracy, the liberals generally champion justice; the conservatives, freedom. If a conservative actually favors liberalism, or a liberal, conservatism, the effect of such bad faith can only be personal since the attainment and perpetuation of both freedom and justice is absolutely necessary for the attainment and perpetuation of human happiness. Accordingly, bad faith makes no substantial effect upon politics in a democracy.

In religion, bad faith can take a variety of forms. A person may believe in God but not belong to any religion. If such a believer believes that one can worship God outside of organized religion, then he or she is not acting in bad faith. But if such a believer believes that one cannot worship God outside of organized religion, then he or she is certainly acting in bad faith. Similarly, a person may believe in God and be a member of a particular religion or denomination but if such a believer is able but unwilling to attend church services, then he or she is also acting in bad faith. Likewise, if such a believer believes that one can only worship God in a religion or denomination that is different from the one to which he or she belongs but does not ever attempt to change his or her membership, then he or she is acting in bad faith. Furthermore, a person may belong to a particular religion but not believe in God: such a nonbeliever may be a hypocrite but not be acting in bad faith; he or she may be acting in bad faith but not be a hypocrite; or he or she may be acting in bad faith while gradually becoming a hypocrite. In all of the situations we have described, the effect of bad faith can only be personal since the practice of religion, despite all of its public manifestations, is essentially a form of subjective experience.

We must observe that wherever a person's concept of God, or of the essence of the absolute and ultimate reality, has been initially formed or subsequently changed as a consequence of the great Universal divine import shift, such a person will not be acting in bad faith unless he or she belongs to a particular religion (where he or she will certainly be acting hypocritically to the extent that he or she is able but unwilling, or willing but unable, to effect a change in the concept of God, or of the essence of the absolute and ultimate reality, in the minds of other believers). In this situation, such a person will be acting in bad faith since he or she is continuing to worship God, or to practice religion in the traditional way, while believing that God, or the essence of the absolute and ultimate reality, is no more than a symbol of existential perfection—the singular idea of the absolute and ultimate objective of human thought and conduct, the supreme ideal which man can esteem, but not the object of worship or of ultimate existential union or reintegration. Again, the effect of such bad faith can only be personal.

Since the effect of bad faith is negligible in politics and causes little more than an uncomfortable personal problem for "believers" in religion, we must turn now to consider its effect on a person's work and interpersonal relationships.

A young man may enter a particular line of work to please his parents, his teachers, or even his closest friends. As he begins to engage in his new work, he finds that he takes little or no pleasure in it and he soon experiences an arising sense of discomposure and repugnance. Nevertheless, he continues to engage in this work because he believes that it is right to fulfill the expectations of other people and he does not believe that he may be justified in seeking work that will be most, or even just more, compatible with his own emerging interpretation of himself and of the world in which he lives; while at the same time he is continuously challenging conventional values and established mores, skeptical of the opinions of others, and mindful of his own intuitions. Consequently, he becomes unhappy with himself, ashamed of himself, angry at himself. He does not believe what he believes and he believes what he does not believe; he does what he does not want to do and he does not do what he wants to do: he is living in bad faith. If he should continue to live in such bad faith throughout the remainder of his life, he will almost certainly fail to attain full personal happiness, even for a moment, and he will most likely fail to attain even the most modest modicum of personal happiness without some degree of additional self-deception.

Likewise, a young woman may decide to enter into an intimate relationship because she believes that such a relationship will bring her lasting personal happiness, and she enters into an intimate relationship with a particular man because she has great faith in him. Soon after the relationship has begun, however, her man's personal conduct and demeanor appear to change and his new actions lead her to believe that he is deliberately attempting to fail to live up to her expectations for him, and she becomes increasingly unhappy. Still, she remains in the relationship because she continues to have faith in him and she does not believe that she will be acting fairly if she becomes disloyal to him; but at the same time she is constantly questioning both her original evaluation of the man and her steadfast commitment to the preservation of the relationship. Of course, she becomes unhappy with herself, ashamed of herself, angry at herself. She does not believe what she believes and she believes what she does not believe; she has made a great mistake but she refuses to attempt to correct it; she is living in bad faith. If she should continue to live in such bad faith until either she or he should die, the outcome will certainly be no better than that in the situation which we have previously described of the young man who is unhappy with his work.

With respect to the fundamental problem in either situation—the effect of bad faith on a person's work or interpersonal relationships—we must uphold our suggestion that religion is not only the original source of bad faith but the sole agent that is actively responsible for the persisting presence of bad faith in human thought and behavior. Under religion, we are required to believe that which we do not know, which we can never come to know, and which by our own efforts is ultimately and absolutely unknowable; under empiricism, and with a good and thorough education, we are required to believe only that which is grounded in knowledge—in knowledge that is derived from experience, in knowledge that is general and not esoteric, in knowledge that precludes divine revelation: herein resides the irreconcilable and intolerable contradiction between reason and faith. The rejection of both monism and theism with the abandonment of both religion and metaphysics will only serve to enhance the acquisition and utilization of knowledge in human affairs and to increase and to broaden human happiness by liberating reason from the inevitable encumbrances of bad faith.

Belief in the supernatural and the practice of religion have served mankind from the first appearance of the species to the present. Religion, with all of its supernatural beings—spirits, angels, demons, gods, and goddesses—was a creation of the human imagination in the service of human emotion—that fear should be less frightful; anger, less furious; happiness, less improbable. The invention of religion was at once the beginning of hope. Notwithstanding, that which has served the species so well for so long no longer confers the benefits of the past but detriments that were unknown in the past because our species had not as yet attained a sufficient level of self-awareness. Until man was able to understand nature, he could not begin to understand himself. Once he had begun to unravel the secrets of nature, he was able to begin to explore the mystery of himself. Then that which was once a source of strength became a cause of weakness. That which once provided hope began to create despair. That which assisted man to overcome a hostile environment prevented man from approaching himself. Even as the child's toy cannot serve as the adult's tool, so the sole delight of our ancestors has become our greatest frustration.

We have offered three reasons for why the persistence of faith in God and the practice of religion now create far more evil than good: one, religion not only fails to prevent war, it is actually a fundamental cause of war; two, religion not only fails to unify mankind, it impugns any rational effort to do so; three, religion not only fails to rectify bad faith, it is undoubtedly the primary cause of bad faith. Accordingly, the future well-being of man and, indeed, perhaps the very survival of life itself on Earth, require that man abandon faith in God—that he abandon Christianity, Islam, and Judaism; that man abandon faith in an ultimate reality that resides within and without the limits of the natural universe—that he abandon Buddhism and Hinduism; and that man abandon faith in all other forms of supernatural beings—that he abandon animism in all of its various guises. We would also avow that the abandonment of faith in God, of faith in the supernatural, and of religious dogma, ritual, and practice indicate not an end but a redefinition and a new beginning of hope.

To conclude our observations with respect to the effects of religion on the progress of human well-being, let us revisit within the history of Western philosophy, from *Les Pensées* by Blaise Pascal, one famous argument for faith in God, namely, Pascal's Wager. Pascal maintained that, if God exists, one who believes in God will win everything and lose nothing, while one who does not believe will win nothing and lose everything; conversely, if God does not exist, neither the believer nor the nonbeliever will lose anything (although, of course, neither one will win anything). But today, we would maintain that the reverse is true. If God does not exist, one who believes in God will win nothing and lose everything, while one who does not believe will win everything and lose nothing. Now, if God exists, the continuing presence of evil in the world appears to indicate that such a God is only benevolent but not omnipotent, since if God were to be omnipotent but not benevolent, God could only be Satan and not be God at all; accordingly, if God exists, the nonbeliever still wins everything and loses nothing, since a benevolent and merciful God cannot punish a good person solely because of his or her unbelief, while the believer still wins nothing and loses everything, since a benevolent and just God cannot reward a believer who is willing but unable to be fully good, for the aforementioned three reasons.

We hold the power to determine our future: a future of self-fulfillment, not of self-destruction, in a human lifetime, not in a life after death, with the best and happiest of consequences both for ourselves and for our posterity. Let us keep faith in reason alone. Let us find courage in truth.

PART II—SYMBOLISM IN ART

We have said that we increase our happiness by taking delight in beauty, whether that of nature or of art. We have also said that everyone and everything that is conducive to the experience of beauty, artistic as well as natural, is always good and desirable, not as a substitute for but as a supplement to all that is instrumental for the satisfaction of our needs and the aversion of our hurts—that the perception and cognition of natural and artistic beauty supplements and reinforces our most elemental pleasure and happiness. We find beauty everywhere in nature and we create or re-create it for ourselves through art. We have concluded that we will always do best to retain the fine arts even though we must discard religion. We would now do well to explain why this should be so. Although we find beauty in nature, the beauty that we experience through the fine arts is of a kind that differs from that of nature in many respects, and the experience of artistic beauty always supplements that of natural beauty. Accordingly, the pleasure and happiness that we derive from the experience of beauty increases and intensifies when we enjoy the beauty of art as well as the beauty of nature. We would now also do well to ask the question, "What is beauty?" To this question, let us venture to reply, "Beauty is a representation of perfection." And what is the meaning of this reply? Well, consider: to exist, we must satisfy the requirements of the law of nature. We must eat and drink. We must clean ourselves and eliminate our wastes. We must avoid injury and sickness or, when this is not possible, we must heal when we become injured and we must get well when we become sick. When we are young and little, we must grow up. When we are old, we must protect our waning health and conserve our ebbing strength. Also, as individuals, we must develop our talents and learn to compensate for our deficiencies. We must overcome our weaknesses and master ourselves. As a species, we must learn to care about each other, to help each other, and to cooperate for the common benefit of all people, of all sentient beings, and of the very biosphere upon which all life upon the earth is dependent. To the extent that we manage all of these affairs with the least possible difficulty, our lives may be said to be either "perfect" or as close as may be possible to our ideal of a life of perfection. Otherwise, our lives are chaos or as close as may be possible to our idea of chaos. Accordingly, the perfect life is rational, orderly, efficient. It is free of hurts, mistakes, wastefulness. As the representation of perfection so defined, beauty also is rational, orderly, efficient. It is free of defect. But the representation is sometimes direct, sometimes indirect. And, in either event, beauty always achieves its lasting effects through symbolism. It is the same whether we are talking about the symbolism of beauty in nature or in art. In nature, beauty is essentially useful. That which is naturally beautiful generally is naturally desirable. The beauty of a natural vista suggests a natural resource that is most likely a very good thing to acquire, to possess, and to make use of. This is how the extraordinary beauty of the fertile plains of France, the lush river valleys and seacoasts of India, or the pristine volcanic islands of Japan, New Zealand, or Hawaii must have first impressed the minds of their permanent settlers who, as likely as not, arrived at their final destination in waves of various size and composition throughout the long evolution of the human species. The beauty of a person of the opposite sex similarly suggests a person who is healthy, strong, and able. Such beauty generates sexual desire and conduces to human procreation. The obvious relationship between the phenomenon of the human sexual physiological urge and the perception of physical beauty in a person of the opposite sex is so widely understood as to require no further elaboration. On a very different level, the symbolism of natural beauty, like that that can generally be said to be true of artistic beauty, may be less obvious and more complex. Then it will be indirect. It will still represent something that is either perfect or, in some way, a component or an agent of that which is perfect. We will devote the remainder of this discourse to a comprehensive discussion of such symbolism.

Let us proceed with a recognition that aesthetics is primarily concerned with refining the means by which we can best frame our understanding of the concept of perfection, or of the ideal, while ethics is concerned with establishing the methodology by which we can best attain (or even just approach) perfection. Hence, the preoccupation with perfection reveals that which is common to both aesthetics and ethics and it thereby reveals the rather loose relationship between the two philosophical disciplines. We could argue that it may be possible for one to become a better person without the necessity of possessing a genuine appreciation of beauty but unlike those who take a more or less puritanical approach to ethics, we will not argue that an appreciation of beauty or a love of the fine arts actually detracts from effective ethical conduct. Rather, we would argue that aesthetics precedes ethics since one must come to know just what one wishes to obtain before one can begin to take the necessary steps to obtain it. Nonetheless, activities within both disciplines are so interdependently critical for the achievement and preservation of human happiness that a preoccupation with those of one to the exclusion of those of the other will almost always tend to create insuperable problems. Accordingly, it is not a question of "either/or" but an acknowledgment of "both/and."

Now let us consider perfection. Perfection is comprised of those human activities and interpersonal relationships that best enable us to satisfy the needs and to avert the hurts of life. We are both aware and happy when we are being successful—by means of the things that we do and the interpersonal relationships that we form—in solving the problems and meeting the demands of human existence. We are aware when our skills are good, when the technology that provides the foundation for our skills is good, when our interpersonal relationships are good, and when the moral code that we must observe to sustain such relationships is good. Perfection consists in the excellence of our behavior and in the harmony of our relationships. The symbolism of much of the beauty of nature and of all of the beauty of the fine arts expresses this perfection. The beauty of form which we perceive in a thing of beauty symbolically expresses the orderliness of efficient work and the amiability of compatible relationships. The beauty of certain aspects of content which we perceive in a thing of beauty likewise symbolically expresses certain aspects associated with, or conducive to, the orderliness of efficient work and the amiability of compatible relationships—for example, a suggestion of such discrete concepts as "acquisition of knowledge," "triumph over adversity," "construction of a grand edifice," "diligence and persistence," "understanding and compassion," "regret and remorse," "solicitude and loving-kindness," or "joy and merrymaking."

It may be tempting for us to attempt to draw a meaningful distinction between spatial art and temporal art but I do not believe that any such distinction is truly relevant to the present discussion. In analyzing the fine arts, we can easily discern that they may be clearly classified into two broad categories: (1) the spatial arts (those the subject or subjects of which, and the communication of the same through some medium of art, essentially occupy space), comprising the visual arts—painting and all other graphic arts, sculpture, and architecture—and (2) the temporal arts (those the subject or subjects of which, and the communication of the same through some medium of art, essentially occupy time), comprising all of the remaining arts—literature, poetry, drama, music, and dance. That one can comprehend a painting within one or two seconds upon first viewing it while one cannot comprehend a twenty-minute long symphony until twenty minutes of listening have elapsed does not preclude that one can increase one's enjoyment of the painting by taking more time to observe the details within it or that one can enjoy various aspects of each of the passages of the symphony as they progress in exact succession according to the design of the composer. Furthermore, that which is represented in one or another of the spatial arts can be effectively represented in one or another of the temporal arts. For example, ten pictures from the 1874 memorial exhibition of the lifework of the Russian painter, designer, and architect Victor Hartman are musically represented in *Pictures at an Exhibition* by Modest Mussorgsky (composed also in 1874), a suite of piano pieces that has been successfully transcribed for symphony orchestra on numerous occasions (most notably by Maurice Ravel in 1922). Examples of the reverse artistic phenomenon, wherein that which is initially represented in one or another of the temporal arts (such as literature) is then effectively represented in one or another of the spatial arts (such as painting) are so commonplace, and have always been commonplace throughout such a long period of time, that no one in particular need be cited at this time.

At this stage in our discussion of symbolism in art, we may do well to offer our opinion with respect to the function of art. We have touched upon this consideration already during our presentation of the introductory premise of the book. We have suggested that the perception and cognition of natural and artistic beauty supplements and reinforces that most elemental pleasure and happiness which we naturally derive from the satisfaction of our needs and the avoidance, prevention, or mitigation of our hurts throughout the inevitable course of human existence. We can conclude, then, that art has a euphoric function since its ultimate object is to contribute to the creation or re-creation of human happiness.

What we are saying should be obvious enough when we consider how we feel when we view a painting like Renoir's *Children on the Seashore at Guernsey*, read a novel like Fielding's *Tom Jones*, or listen to a piece of music like Mozart's Symphony No. 27, but what are we to say about the way we feel when we view a painting like Picasso's *Guernica*, read a novel like Goethe's *The Sorrows of Young Werther*, or listen to a piece of music like Tchaikowsky's Symphony No. 6? In these instances, we still derive a feeling of overall satisfaction but the pathway to this result involves much that is intellectually indirect, intense, enigmatic, complex, and profound. In these instances, the euphoric function of art draws heavily upon either or both of the two great theories of classical aesthetics, Platonic didacticism and Aristotelian catharsis. Let us digress for a moment to explain how these theories are relevant to, and form a part of, the euphoric function of art. Through didacticism, we are able to learn (by observing the mistakes made by others) how either to avoid or to resolve many of the problems of life. Through catharsis, our pleasure—arising in the vicarious experience of a work of art, such as a tragedy (whether depicted as such in a drama, a painting, or a piece of music)—is not that that is gained through the symbolic satisfaction of needs but that that proceeds from the actual alleviation of emotional pain. The depiction of tragedy arouses certain uncomfortable or even painful emotions, such as anger, fear, or remorse, and also certain sympathetic emotions, such as pity, awe, or compassion, and the assuagement of the uncomfortable or painful emotion concurring with the intensification of the sympathetic emotion provides us with a singular kind of pleasure not unlike that that comes about when we take an analgesic for a headache, apply a soothing salve to a burn, or rest in a soft armchair after taking a long and strenuous hike through the woods. Like the Roman poet Horace (who argued in his *Ars poetica* that the function of art is both to please and to instruct), we would argue that the didactic and cathartic functions of art, to the extent that they may be present together in works of art, are equally valid. Wherever one appears independently and exclusively of the other, its particular artistic function will still remain valid to some degree but its aesthetic effectiveness will be greatly diminished. For example, a work of literature or drama in the genre of horror may have substantial cathartic value although it will just as likely have little or no didactic value. Similarly, any morality play that fails to arouse the emotions of its viewers will quickly fall flat and will surely fail (in the absence of some form of extraneous assistance) to attract a substantial audience for its intended message.

We can see, then, that all art that has a cathartic or a didactic function has a euphoric function, albeit of a particular kind, but not all art that has a euphoric function has a cathartic or a didactic function. When times are good—when people are secure, healthy, and prosperous—when the problems of human existence are almost negligible, the incidence of the presence of the cathartic and didactic functions of art in works of art is minimal; when reverse situations prevail, the incidence of the presence of the cathartic and didactic functions of art in works of art becomes maximal. In all events, art has an incontrovertible euphoric function—to increase human happiness wherever happiness and equanimity are already present, and otherwise to provide relief, comfort, and hope in the face of anxiety and misery.

An analysis of symbolism in a work of art reveals two kinds or levels of symbolism, the symbolism of detail (which, in general, involves a number of symbols) and the symbolism of overall composition (in which, in general, a single, dominant, and unifying theme either is immediately evident or eventually attracts the attention of the perceiver). We may call the symbolism of the former kind "microsymbolism" and that of the latter, "macrosymbolism." Symbolism of either kind may further be classified according to whether it is conventional (meaning that the symbolism is commonly understood and frequently employed, especially within a given culture) or nonconventional (meaning that while the symbolism is generally intelligible, its use by one or another artist is novel or unique and consequently its interpretations, at least initially if not in the long run, may be somewhat vague and multifarious). Since, of all the fine arts, my understanding of (and fondness for) music is greatest, I will presently commit the greater portion of this discourse to an interpretive discussion of nonconventional macrosymbolism in music. Beforehand, however, I would like to provide some brief comments with respect to various aspects of symbolism in all of the fine arts.

Let us proceed by first considering the import of symbolism as it appears in the graphic arts, those arts exclusively concerned with the expression of ideas (and the consequent arousal of associated feelings) in space rather than with expression of ideas in time or in some combination of space and time. We will confine our remarks to six famous paintings.

Raphael's *St. George and the Dragon* is a symbol of the triumph of good over evil. The dragon, like the feathered serpent or the unicorn, is a mythical animal, commonly comprised of a serpent's body, a bird's wings, a lion's claws, and a crocodile's head. In China, the dragon has always functioned as a symbol of power, fertility, and good fortune, but in the conventional symbolism of the Western world, it has always been, like the serpent which forms the greater portion of its body, an unmistakable symbol of evil, just as the image of St. George mounted upon his horse is a symbol of good.

El Greco's *View of Toledo*, with its unearthly aura surrounding the city as seen on the occasion of a dark and frightful storm, is a symbol of awesome supernatural power. The modern viewer's sense of this power is so fully overwhelming and terrifying that that which originally was conceived of as the divine source of this power now almost seems more demonic than divine.

Rembrandt's *The Return of the Prodigal Son* is a symbol of reconciliation. On the level of microsymbolism, the figure of the kneeling boy in this painting can be seen as a symbol of obeisance. On the other hand, Overbeck's *Joseph Being Sold by his Brothers* is a symbol of betrayal. With both of these paintings, the visual arts are allied with literature and the power of the symbolism is intensified in direct proportion to the extent that the viewer has a familiarity with the related Bible story.

Van Gogh's *The Starry Night* is somewhat more difficult to understand than the paintings we have mentioned thus far. He portrays a village being seen at nighttime from an elevated position (most likely a hilltop or a hillside) but the appearance of the stars in the sky above the village has an explosive, violent, and threatening quality in stark contrast to the orderly, tranquil, and comforting quality that we usually sense when we actually view a starry sky at nighttime. To my way of thinking, then, the painting is a symbol of disillusionment, but I readily admit that some readers may take issue with this interpretation.

Finally, perhaps we can all agree that Picasso's *Guernica* is a symbol of the horror of war. In this painting, it is noteworthy that the artist seems to achieve his macrosymbolism through the magnitude and intensity of his microsymbolism. Some examples of these symbols, with their patent imports, include: a woman holding her dead child, symbolizing anguish; another woman trapped in a burning building, terror; a bull, raw power; a dying horse, agony; a dead warrior, death; the sun hidden behind a light bulb, the abuse of reason; and a hand holding a lantern (at the center of the painting), the uselessness of reason at a time and place of savage brutality.

We have seen that the use of symbolism—of microsymbolism in the detail and of macrosymbolism for the overall effect—in the spatial fine arts—in painting, sculpture, architecture, and other related fine arts that rely upon an immediate visual impression—conveys a meaning behind the obvious images—by presenting for recollection the ideas of certain values and/or ideologies which are held and cherished by the artist and which may, to some degree, be familiar to the perceiver. We have also noted that the symbolism may either be conventional or nonconventional, depending upon whether or not a tradition has been established for the common use of the symbolism.

The use of symbolism in the other fine arts is very much the same, except that the medium by which ideas are conveyed provides an eventual, rather than an immediate, mental impression. In these fine arts, ideas are presented over time rather than in space. The microsymbols of the temporal fine arts—of literature, drama, music, dance, and other related fine arts that rely upon the elapse of a given, albeit sometimes a somewhat variable, length of time during which the relevant work is presented—are generally introduced one by one, but as the work progresses, all or some of them may be presented simultaneously to create in the perceiver a striking mental impression and a powerful emotional reaction. The cognition of the macrosymbolism in any given work of the temporal fine arts cannot occur, of course, until the elapse of the time that may be required for the complete perception of the work. Hence, any sense of the macrosymbolism of a particular Chopin piano piece will not be fully apprehended by the listener until the conclusion of the performance time of, say, four or five minutes, while a full understanding of the macrosymbolism of Proust's great novel *Remembrance of Things Past* will not emerge until the reader has finished reading all of the seven parts that comprise this author's unitary oeuvre, an accomplishment that, for some readers, might occur after the elapse of only a few days but that, for others, might require the elapse of several weeks or months.

Let us take a moment or two to offer a few comments with respect to the import of microsymbolism as it appears among various examples of great literature and music. For the former, we will consider three well-known novels of various nineteenth and twentieth century European authors; for the latter, three well-known symphonic poems by the German romantic composer Richard Strauss.

Dostoyevsky's *Crime and Punishment* is replete with microsymbolism at many levels of meaning but perhaps the most telling is the symbol of the thirty silver roubles. The central character of the novel, Raskolnikov, murders an old woman moneylender for "thirty silver roubles." The old woman is described as not only unworthy and worthless but evil. (Indeed, the very use of the microsymbol "moneylender" introduces by way of the power of suggestion the same import.) Raskolnikov plans to use the stolen money first to assist his mother and his sister, and then to finance the completion of his studies at St. Petersburg University. Thus, Raskolnikov attempts at once to justify to himself his enormous crime and his rejection of the Christian moral values which his Russian society has long adopted. The image of the "thirty silver roubles" clearly calls to mind the "thirty pieces of silver" for which Judas Iscariot betrayed Jesus in the Garden of Gethsemane on the Mount of Olives. Accordingly, the thirty silver roubles may be seen as a symbol of Raskolnikov's rejection of Jesus' way of meeting the difficulties of human existence.

Flaubert's *Madame Bovary* tells the tragic story of a rather foolish woman who, in her personal relationships with men, constantly rejects the one who is hers to have, and constantly seeks others who ultimately elude her grasp. The woman not only is dishonest with others, she is dishonest with herself. She is a victim of *malvais fois* for, to paraphrase our meaning in the language of Sartre, "she does not believe what she believes and she believes what she does not believe." Hence, at the very moment when the opportunity to attain lasting happiness is at hand, she mysteriously appears to fall into a state of ennui and, as a consequence, she seeks to gain her freedom, albeit a kind of freedom that inevitably leads to her own self-destruction. Perhaps the most powerful among a number of microsymbols that Flaubert uses to convey some idea of this sense of personal freedom is that of an open window in a room that is otherwise too small, extremely confining, and insidiously stifling.

With a narrative more often in the style of lyrical poetry than of descriptive prose, Hesse's *Siddhartha* tells the story of the young son of a Brahmin and his lifelong search for truth. In the course of his wanderings, Siddhartha meets Siddhartha Guatama, the Buddha, whose given name he shares. Now, in my opinion, the novel undertakes to identify the idea of love as the synthesis of all of the truth that may be common to Christianity and Buddhism. The image of the river, which recurs frequently throughout the story of Siddhartha's life, is a compelling microsymbol of truth—of the intersection between samsara and nirvana, between suffering and release, and, in the final analysis, between Buddhahood with a remainder and Buddhahood without a remainder. But on a different level of thinking, the river is also—as the microsymbol of truth—a microsymbol of the intersection between ignorance and knowledge, between malevolence and benevolence, and, again in the final analysis, between endless particular conflict and lasting universal peace.

When we think of music as one of the fine arts, we generally think of "art music" or "serious music" as opposed to "folk music" and "popular music." Such music is customarily allocated among various categories according to its origin in space and time so that, by way of examples, we may have Italian music, German music, French music, Russian music, and so on, and we may also have Renaissance music, baroque music, classical music, romantic music, and modern (or contemporary) music. To provide a description of a particular kind of music as precisely as possible, the spatial and temporal categories are usually combined so that we have Italian Renaissance music, French baroque music, Viennese classical music, German romantic music, Russian contemporary music, and so on. The term "classical music" is a misnomer when it is used (as it often is) as a substitute for the terms "art music" and "serious music" since it properly identifies the music of the Viennese school during the classical period (1750-1825) and specifically refers to the music of Haydn, Mozart, and early Beethoven.

Serious music may also be categorized according to whether or not it is "absolute music," meaning that it stands on its own merits without relying upon any association with any of the other fine arts. Music that cannot be said to be "absolute music" generally includes vocal music, opera, ballet, and "program music." These kinds of music either combine with other fine arts, such as with literature or drama, or they convey pictorial or poetic ideas in sound, generally by association with or influence of extramusical sources.

The foregoing comments have been offered simply in an attempt to provide some helpful background for the musical portion of our discussion. Before we examine the three Strauss selections, we would also do well to consider the methodology and technique for the use of microsymbolism in music.

The simplest way for a composer to create or to re-create a microsymbol in his or her music is to imitate a music-like sound from an extramusical source. For example, the call of the cuckoo can be easily imitated by writing a falling major third for a middle range woodwind instrument, such as the clarinet. This was done by Beethoven with great success in his Symphony No. 6 (the Pastorale), near the end of the second movement ("Scene by the Brook"), where he also imitates the calls of the nightingale and the quail and combines the three bird call imitations in a peaceful cadenza for an extraordinarily beautiful effect that provides a telling microsymbol of rustic nature. Other examples of imitations (and related connotations) include: bells (religion, ceremonial occasions, victory, etc.); trumpet fanfares (the military, battle, summons, etc.); horn calls (the hunt); the gong (death).

Another way for a composer to create or to re-create a microsymbol in his or her music is to quote music from another source. For example, a national anthem may be quoted to suggest the nation or nationality associated with the anthem. Tchaikowsky quoted the French and the Russian national anthems to identify the opposing armies in the 1812 Overture, and Puccini quoted the American national anthem to identify Lieutenant B. F. Pinkerton, U.S.N. in *Madame Butterfly*. For another example, a composer may create or re-create a microsymbol of impending doom by quoting the well-known initial phrases of the medieval plainsong Dies irae from the Requiem mass of the Roman liturgy. Berlioz did so with great effect in his Symphonie fantastique, as did also Rachmaninoff in his Variations on a Theme of Paganini for piano and orchestra.

When music is combined with drama, as in an opera or a ballet, the microsymbolism of the integrated artistic presentation can derive, at least in part, from the theatrical set, scenery, costumery, and lighting of the drama. In Act One of Puccini's *La Bohème*, for example, the two lit candles of Mimi and Rodolfo present a microsymbol of life and love; subsequently, the two unlit candles, of impending death and grief.

A composer can also create or re-create a microsymbol in his or her music by musical suggestion of extramusical ideas. I will now offer numerous examples of melodic, harmonic, rhythmic, and timbral sounds (and related connotations): diatonic melodic progressions (security, tranquility, happiness, etc.); whole tone melodic progressions (mystery, softness, delicacy, etc.); sweeping scales, either ascending or descending, whether diatonic or chromatic (exuberance, ardor, fury, etc.); open fifth harmonic combinations (power); open tritone harmonic combinations (antipathy, conflict, aggression, etc.); diminished seventh chords—chords in which adjacent tones are always a minor third apart (mystery, drama, intrigue, etc.); augmented fifth chords—chords in which adjacent tones are always a major third apart (mystery, softness, delicacy, etc.); melodic and harmonic progressions superimposed upon a pedal point (power, majesty, profundity, etc.); even rhythmic patterns (security, tranquility, happiness, etc.); dotted or double-dotted rhythmic patterns—rhythmic patterns of an uneven kind such that a sound with three or seven temporal units is followed by a sound with one temporal unit (honor, elegance, stateliness, etc.); string timbre (warmth, richness, expressiveness, etc.); flute timbre (purity, clarity, simplicity, etc.); clarinet timbre (mellowness, richness, expressiveness, etc.); double reed instrument timbre—that of the oboe, English horn, and bassoon (pungency, incisiveness, melancholy, etc.); conical bore instrument timbre—that of the horn and tuba (power, nobleness, heroism, etc.); cylindrical bore instrument timbre—that of the trumpet and trombone (power, incisiveness, solemnness, etc.). Since melodic, harmonic, rhythmic, and timbral sounds can be presented within a range of combinations from the most simple to the most complex, the composer can create or re-create a microsymbol with varying degrees of intensity. Furthermore, if the composer intends that a particular musical microsymbol should take on a distinct character which will necessarily recur throughout the musical composition, he or she will introduce it as a fundamental leitmotif that can be modified in various ways over the course of the music to conform with the development of personalities, the dramatic action of situations as they may arise, or the nuances of general ideas, specific interpretations, and associated emotions.

We would be remiss if we should fail to mention how a composer can also use tempo (the fastness or slowness of the music), dynamics (the loudness or softness of the music), and changes in tempo and/or dynamics—whether gradual or abrupt—to suggest extramusical ideas. Here are some examples (and related connotations): fast music (energy, excitement, activity, etc.); slow music (relaxation, contemplation, tranquility, etc.); loud music (power, conflict, awe, etc.); soft music (delicacy, tranquility, compassion, etc.); accelerando and/or crescendo (increasing tension, excitement and drama); ritardando and/or decrescendo (decreasing tension, subsiding energy, and generally a change of mood).

Another kind of musical microsymbol is that of the musical "narrator." This symbolic device is used much in the same manner as the first person or third person narrator in a novel who relates the story and offers personal comments from time to time with respect to the plot, the characters, and the significant interrelationships of the characters. The narrator may introduce the work, may establish his or her point of view at various intervals throughout the work, and may provide an epilogue, or he or she may be involved in but a few, or even in only one or another, of any successive phases of detached commentary. Three outstanding examples of the effective use of the musical "narrator" include: the soft orchestral conclusion to Act Two (immediately following the Night Watchman's song) of Wagner's *Die Meistersinger von Nürnberg*, where the orchestra seems to be excusing (with compassion and serenity, as though possessing the perspective of a highly detached and extraordinarily discerning observer) the tumultuous riot that erupted among the townspeople before the unfortunate Sixtus Beckmesser could conclude his noisy and outrageous serenade; the matter-of-fact promenade theme that introduces and recurs throughout Mussorgsky's *Pictures at an Exhibition* for piano (or for orchestra, if one is listening to one of the orchestral transcriptions of the original composition, such as the well-known one by Ravel); and the simple brief orchestral passages which open the first movement, open and close the second movement, and open the third movement of Tchaikowsky's Violin Concerto.

Let us summarize our discussion of microsymbolism in music by presenting exemplars from the three symphonic poems of Richard Strauss of which we spoke.

In the section "The Hero's Battlefield" of *Ein Heldenleben* ("A Hero's Life"), Strauss provides a microsymbol of battle by imitating the trumpet fanfares that one might expect to hear in a military camp. The fanfares are presented three times—the first, very soft, as though from a great distance (three trumpet players are directed to play from a room located offstage); the second, a little louder, as though approaching closer (the players are directed to play from the wings); the third, very loud, as though from at hand (the players are directed to return onstage and to play from their usual positions in the orchestra). Each of the fanfare episodes is preceded by orchestral "narrator" commentary at a level of volume and intensity that approximates, or increases by turns to approximate, that of the respective fanfare. The dramatic effect is extraordinarily powerful and deeply moving.

In *Till Eulenspiegel's Merry Pranks*, Strauss introduces his musical representation of the title character with a quiet "once upon a time" orchestral passage that suggests the onset of the narration of a farcical fairy tale or legend. The presence of the musical "narrator" is strikingly vivid at one point during the course of the tone poem where it appears to be passing judgment on Till Eulenspiegel for the violent excesses of his mischievous antics. The musical "narrator" then appears one more time following an episode that portrays the trial and execution of the prankster to bring the tone poem to a lighthearted and playful conclusion.

In *Don Quixote*, Strauss uses all of the ways to create or to re-create musical microsymbolism which we have discussed, with the two exceptions of quotation of music from other sources and of microsymbolism borrowed from related fine arts (inasmuch as the images suggested by the great Cervantes novel upon which the symphonic poem is based are not visually depicted by means of the dramatic presentation of an opera or a ballet). On one occasion, Strauss imitates the bleating of sheep; on another, through the use of a wind machine, an imaginary flight through the air when Don Quixote, suffering from a distorted perception that he is about to vanquish giants, charges (and then becomes entangled in) the rotating sails of a tower windmill. Strauss uses leitmotifs and the distinct timbres of solo string instruments to identify the principal characters—the cello and a serious resolute theme for Don Quixote; the viola and an amiable easygoing theme for Sancho Panza; the violin and a noble, even a sublime, theme for the Lady Dulcinea. He creates a poignant musical microsymbol of the death of Don Quixote by writing a quiet, unassuming, and almost apologetic descending glissando for the solo cello close to the end of the composition. Finally, providing the same kind of musical microsymbolism that he uses in *Till Eulenspiegel's Merry Pranks*, Strauss scores a straightforward dispassionate orchestral passage to close the tone poem that is identical to the one that he uses to open it, thus creating a musical "narrator" to frame the musical portrayal of the plot, characters, and interrelationships of the novel.

We have said that once a person has fully experienced any given work of the temporal fine arts—once a person has read a novel from the first word to the last, or has listened to a symphony from the beginning to the end—he or she can grasp a sense of the macrosymbolism of the work. We have also said that macrosymbolism is the symbolism of overall composition in which, generally speaking, a single, dominant, and unifying theme is present. Such a theme indirectly expresses one or another of various aspects of our mundane efforts to satisfy our needs and to allay our hurts. But our apprehension of the import of the symbol arouses within us emotions that are quite similar to those that accompany the actual experiences—whether the experiences of thought, reflection, planning, action, or reaction—of our lives. Since all art arouses within us either agreeable emotions or disagreeable emotions that either immediately resolve into agreeable ones or attend an idea that has as its object the communication of some kind of understanding that can only lead to future agreeable emotions, we say that art essentially has a euphoric function and sometimes also a cathartic function and/or a didactic function. And since the images of literature (and of most of the forms of the temporal fine arts, with the exception of absolute music, since most of these forms, with the exception of absolute music, are dependent upon literature) are directly communicated, the macrosymbolism of the various forms of the temporal fine arts, except for that of absolute music, generally is conventional. Thus, we can rightfully speak of three broad categories of macrosymbolism in the temporal fine arts (even without excluding absolute music, for a reason which we will soon reveal), closely following the three traditional categories of literature, that of the epic or drama, that of tragedy, and that of comedy. (Or it may follow some combination of the traditional literary categories, such as the tragicomedy.) Our encounters with such works of art are vicarious experiences—we feel joy and happiness, and sometimes exuberance and mirth, or we learn from a story of the errors and shortcomings of others, even while we may feel compassion and pity for the grief, remorse, or nostalgia of others.

The images of absolute music are not communicated as directly as those of the other temporal fine arts. The interpretation of the import of symbols is more subjective. In my opinion, the emotions aroused upon the perception of a work of absolute music are stronger than those aroused upon the perception of a work of literature or drama but not as strong as those aroused upon the perception of a work of music associated in some way with a natural phenomenon or with a literary work or a work of one of the visual arts. This is a very subjective statement, of course; in all instances, it assumes that the talents of the creative artists (and, if and where applicable, of the performing artists as well) are comparable. For me, vis-à-vis my perception of any sample within the entire range of the various kinds of fine arts, my perception of music in any of its various forms elicits the stronger emotional reaction, and it is all the stronger wherever the burden imposed upon my imagination is least demanding.

As for the macrosymbolism of absolute music, I would submit that it is much the same as the macrosymbolism of the other temporal fine arts (although it is far less obvious), for the composer is telling a story, *his* (or *her*) story, a story written in notes and translated into tones, a story expressed through the alternative language of music, a language a little less precise and a little more emotional than any of the verbal languages, but a language nevertheless. The story, then, can be none other than one more epic or drama, one more tragedy, or one more comedy (or tragicomedy). And if the musical "story" is transmitted in a language that is less objective than verbal language, then the ways that it may be received and interpreted will likely be euphoric but multifarious.

Since I believe that the import of the macrosymbolism of literary works (and of all other works of the temporal fine arts that are inspired by, and consequently dependent upon, literary works) is already generally obvious, I would like to devote the remainder of the present section to a subjective analysis of macrosymbolism as it appears to me in each of seven compositions of absolute music which I have selected from the oeuvres of Mozart, Beethoven, Mendelssohn, Tchaikowsky, and Rachmaninoff. It is my sincere hope that these analyses will not fail to sustain the interest of all who have remained with me up to this point.

The first composition which we shall consider is Mozart's Concerto for Flute and Harp in C Major, K. 299. This piece was written in 1778 for the Count of Guines, a cultivated French aristocrat who played the flute, and his talented daughter who played the harp. It is written in the conventional concerto form of the day—a fast opening movement in concerto-sonata form, a slow middle movement and a fast rondo finale.

We have said that "the beauty of certain aspects of content which we perceive in a thing of beauty . . . symbolically expresses certain aspects associated with, or conducive to, the orderliness of efficient work and the amiability of compatible relationships." Now, it is with "the amiability of compatible relationships" that we are presently concerned and it is the amiability of compatible relationships of a particular kind which we find so easily in the Concerto for Flute and Harp. For me, this piece is a symbolic presentation of the story of a happy childhood, where the music of the flute symbolizes the child, that of the harp symbolizes the continuous love and tireless support of the child's parents, and that of the orchestra symbolizes the dependable friendship and goodwill of the community within which the family lives and interacts. Since the story is a drama of light and amusing character with an obviously happy ending, we can safely assert that the macrosymbolism of the concerto falls within the category of comedy. Our experience upon listening to this music provides us with a feeling of happiness as we come to sense the joyful feelings associated with a wonderful child who is being raised by loving parents in a warm and supportive social environment. The overall theme of the macrosymbolism of the concerto may be said to be solicitude and loving-kindness, which is particularly felt in the slow movement. Furthermore, the rondo refrain of the finale suggests that solicitude and loving-kindness must ultimately and inevitably overflow into joy and merrymaking. Let us proceed now to follow the presentation and development of the macrosymbolism of the concerto by briefly analyzing the music of each movement in turn.

In Movement One—Allegro, the mood of the music is light and cheerful. The first theme introduces the parents as well as the community in which the happy couple make their home. With the repeat of the exposition, the child itself is introduced in the company of its parents. By the time that the second theme commences, the child has begun to take on an independent identity from that of its parents—we could say that the child appears to have "come into one's own." For me, the music of the entire first movement—through the exposition, development and recapitulation—symbolizes the intellectual development of the child, which is to say in particular, that the music symbolizes the story of the life of the child as a student at school. The orchestra symbolizes the teachers who guide and train the child while the harp symbolizes the parents who encourage and assist the child with his or her studies. The progress of the education appears almost effortless and flawless inasmuch as the teachers are competent and conscientious, the child is bright and receptive, and the parents are loving and supportive.

In Movement Two—Andantino, the music is much quieter, the orchestra unobtrusive, and the interaction between flute and harp considerably more pronounced. The mood is serene and loving. For me, the music of the second movement symbolizes a family day spent together at home—as on a Saturday, a Sunday, or a holiday—a day of intimate family life characterized by peaceful and tender interpersonal relationships. In the second half of the songlike theme, Mozart writes a brief sequence of exquisite beauty that symbolizes both the endurance of familial love and the power of parental nurture. The sequence recurs throughout the movement and it is one of those extraordinary passages—like, for example, the similar one in the slow movement of the Mozart Clarinet Concerto—that makes the listener who has heard it before yearn with enormous anticipated pleasure to hear one more time either a live or a recorded performance of the composition in which the passage is contained.

In Movement Three—Rondeau: Allegro, the mood of the music once again is light and cheerful. The rondo refrain, as we have already intimated, is particularly exuberant and playful. The episodes between the rondo refrain are also quite spirited and Mozart writes repeated phrases within brief sequences for some of them which symbolize the endurance of love. The rapid succession of light and cheerful tunes—most of which, like the rondo refrain itself, recur at least one time—symbolize the variety of additional activities in which the child participates or engages—playing with friends, joining a sports team, taking private lessons, practicing a skill, visiting with relatives, shopping with parents, eating at a restaurant, and so forth—each activity being strongly supported by the child's parents and, to a certain extent, even by the community in which the family lives and interacts.

I do not intend to suggest that only those happy children who are always strongly loved by their parents and only those loving parents who are presently raising happy children can fully appreciate this composition (although such persons must certainly be counted among those most likely to be drawn to the music), since anyone who enjoys close and enduring family relationships can hardly fail to apprehend the macrosymbolism of this music and thereby access a source of enormous supplemental pleasure and happiness. I also do not intend to suggest that my interpretation of the macrosymbolism of this composition is the only one that is cogent or even that any person who appreciates this music must be fully aware of its macrosymbolism since, in the latter respect, I believe that the symbolism of a thing of beauty (like that of a dream) is at first experienced unconsciously by the human mind.

The second composition which we shall consider is also written by Mozart. It is the Symphony No. 39 in E-Flat Major, K. 543. It is at once one of Mozart's greatest creations and one of the greatest symphonies ever written throughout the entire history of music. It has always been my favorite composition of all of Mozart's wonderful music. As is well known, Mozart composed his last three symphonies, Nos. 39-41, in the early part of the summer of 1788, approximately three and a half years before his death.

The symphony is in four movements: a moderately-fast opening movement with an impressive slow introduction, a quiet slow movement, a conventional dance movement (the minuet) that is repeated following a simple and proportional interlude (the trio), and a fast finale. Now, in my way of thinking, the beauty which we perceive when we listen to this symphony is much like that which we perceive when we listen to the Concerto for Flute and Harp. In both compositions the beauty which we perceive symbolically expresses the amiability of compatible relationships. However, whereas the concerto symbolically expresses a love between unequals (the love of the parents and the other members of the community for the child, and that of the child for its parents and the other members of the community), the symphony symbolically expresses a love between equals. For me, the symphony is a symbolic presentation of the story of a close friendship. Also, unlike the listener's immediate awareness of the composer's treatment of the flute, the harp and the orchestra in the concerto, the tone colors of the various musical instruments brought to bear in the symphony (with the possible exception of the first clarinet and the flute in the trio of the third movement, as we shall see in due course) do not readily appear to take on any special symbolic significance. Notwithstanding the poignant quality of the introduction or of the second theme of the slow movement, the overall effect of the music of the symphony, like that of the concerto, is light and pleasant. Also, like the concerto, the symphony has an obviously happy ending. Accordingly, the music of the symphony, like that of the concerto, may be interpreted as a symbolic presentation of a story that can only be appropriately classified as a comedy. Let us turn now to consider the particular macrosymbolism of the music of each movement as we attempt to see how the general story of this friendship arises and unfolds.

In Movement One—Adagio—Allegro, the slow introduction is sonorous, noble and self-contained. For me, this music seems to introduce a solitary person, a person who possesses integrity and self-esteem, who is almost entirely self-sufficient, and who is regarded almost as a hero in the eyes of others. While this person will soon be identified with another in an intimate friendship throughout the remainder of the symphony, the friendship at the outset exists only as a potentiality, that is, as the inevitable effect of a powerful human need and a growing personal desire. As the introduction progresses, the listener can recognize that this person—although he or she cannot in any sense be regarded as an inferior or incomplete person—suffers intensely. This person suffers from a heavy weariness, from the enormous stresses of his or her life, and from an abiding loneliness. The first of these three distinct impressions is conveyed through the labored progress of the music. The second and third are conveyed through the microsymbolism of discordant harmonies, of a sforzando diatonic seventh chord in first inversion by the full orchestra in the instance of the impression of emotional stress and by the sound of a quiet, simple and exposed augmented fourth interval—the most dissonant harmonic interval in music except for the minor second and one that neither Mozart again nor any other composer of his day ever uses in such a manner—in the instance of the impression of loneliness. The stuporous sound of the exposed augmented fourth interval then quickly gives way to a cadential six-four chord which links the introduction to the exposition.

The Allegro itself is most pleasant inasmuch as the head of the first theme is based upon little more than the ascending broken E-flat tonic triad in root position followed by a partially ascending and then partially descending broken B-flat dominant triad (also, as it turns out, in root position). Accordingly, all of the previous tension of the music disappears. Of even greater microsymbolic import, the head of the first theme is presented as a three-note subject followed by its direct imitation at the octave. This kind of sound clearly suggests an agreeable, albeit tentative, dialogue between two persons, which is to say that it suggests the beginning of a friendship. Now, the characteristic mode of personal conduct at the beginning of a friendship consists of the attempts by one person to come to an understanding of another person and, by way of reciprocity, the second person's attempts to come to an understanding of the first. Accordingly, we may say that the first theme of the Allegro symbolizes the mutual efforts of two new friends to obtain some understanding of each other.

The music of the second theme is at once more confident and more animated than that of the first theme. We may say that it symbolizes at the very least the successful efforts of either of the friends to encourage the other and at best the successful efforts of both friends to encourage each other.

So much for the symbolism of friendship in the first movement. Before we proceed to consider the music of the remaining movements, we would offer the following comments in interpretation of the remaining music of the first movement. The repeat of the exposition symbolizes a reflection in the memory (that is, in the memories of the two friends) of all that has transpired between the friends during the exposition. The development section, which is essentially based upon the music of the second theme, symbolizes the growing mutual encouragement of the friends as they approach life together. The recapitulation symbolically reinforces the concepts and acts of continuous mutual understanding and continual mutual encouragement in friendship.

In Movement Two—Andante con moto, the quiet mood of the opening theme suggests that the friends are alone together in a relaxed setting. In my opinion, the predominant movement by steps of the opening theme suggests that the friends are coming to know one another in a more intimate manner. Mozart's use of the harmonic minor to harmonize a repetition of the head of the theme toward the close of the opening section seems to hint of a possibility of impendent trouble for the relationship. A brief modulation to the relative minor leads to a stormy second theme but the confinement of this theme to the violins in the upper register suggests not a dialogue (that is, not a quarrel between the friends) but a heartfelt confession of a recent or present indiscretion and betrayal. The music continues with a passage that reminisces the middle portion of the opening theme but this amiable interlude is interrupted with another passionate outburst. The passage that follows this is one of tender and exquisite beauty—a short, fugue-like passage once again in the tonality of the opening theme that symbolizes the close reciprocity of the friends at this juncture: the contrite confessor seems to be grievously apologizing and imploringly begging for pardon while, alternately, the injured confidant seems to be tenderly comforting the offender and nobly dismissing the freely-disclosed offence. The repetitive exchange culminates in a grand outpouring of harmonious resolution that symbolizes the complete pardon of the offence and the immediate reconciliation of the friends.

The second movement is written in a modified song form that may be designated by the formula ABABA. The repeat of the first and second themes of this movement, like the repeat of the exposition of the first movement, symbolizes a conscious reflection upon the symbolic events of the second movement. The second repetition of the first theme, which represents an approach to a deeper level of concern for another person and which closes with a peaceful codetta, symbolically reinforces the concepts and acts of understanding and forgiveness in friendship.

Movement Three—Menuetto Allegretto-Trio is a simple dance in ¾ meter (the minuet), the repetition of which is separated by an even simpler dance interlude for three instruments (the trio). The movement, like all minuets with trios, is written in song form (ABA). As an historical note, the minuet originated at the court of Louis XIV of France around 1650 and it gradually became popular among all of the aristocracy throughout Europe by 1750. The minuet-and-trio became the conventional next-to-last movement for most of the various compositions written in sonata form during the classical period of German music (1750-1830).

The music of the minuet symbolizes sociability. It suggests that the two friends may be participating in the dance with other couples or, in any event, that they are enjoying each other's company in some kind of a social setting. In the minuet, the happiness of the friends is indistinguishable from that of the other participants and the discrete quality of their special relationship is not conspicuous except during the trio.

The music of the trio symbolizes their close companionship. The trio is written in a kind of miniature modified song form (ABABA). The main section is scored for two clarinets and a flute performing as a trio against a background of very soft but rhythmic chords sounded by the strings. One of the clarinets provides an accompaniment of arpeggios for the melody of the other. This melody represents one of the friends. The melody consists of two successive phrases. (At the outset, the two phrases are repeated. Later, during the two times when the main section recurs, they are not repeated.) At the pause between the ending of each phrase and the beginning of the next, the flute—which represents the other friend—directly imitates the second half of the phrase. It is this imitation that so clearly suggests the closeness—the inseparability—the oneness of the two friends. The intervening section is scored for strings and it serves in its turn as a microsymbol for a detached narrator who seems to look down upon the happy proceedings and to offer (as it were) a kind of unobtrusive approbation.

In Movement Four—Finale. Allegro, the music fully develops the concept of the oneness of the friends that was briefly hinted during the course of the trio of the preceding movement. The first seven notes of the head of the first theme are so employed as a recurring and unifying motif throughout the movement as to suggest the unanimity and constancy or, in perhaps the most appropriate choice of words, the loyalty of the friendship. That the friendship endures, notwithstanding the manifold and multifarious experiences of life, is clearly symbolized at the end of the movement when Mozart writes a descending harmonic sequence that passes through every diatonic tonality. In my opinion, this passage symbolizes the entire range of the various experiences of a lifetime, however long it may endure. Immediately following this passage, Mozart concludes his great symphony with two quick successive restatements—rather than a single restatement—of the seven-note head of the first theme. Once again in my opinion, such a conclusion symbolizes the steadfast loyalty of two friends locked in an indestructible relationship.

At this point, let us recall once again what we have said concerning the symbolism of beauty: "the beauty of certain aspects of content which we perceive in a thing of beauty . . . symbolically expresses certain aspects associated with, or conducive to, the orderliness of efficient work and the amiability of compatible relationships." As we turn to a subjective analysis of the macrosymbolism of two symphonies of Beethoven, the fifth and the ninth, our concern will also turn to the signification of "the orderliness of efficient work." Since each symphony, like many other of Beethoven's compositions, has a heroic quality and conveys some sense of a heroic struggle, the music of each may be properly interpreted as a symbolic presentation of a story that can only be appropriately classified as an epic. As I see it, the music of the Fifth Symphony is a symbol of "triumph over adversity," that of the Ninth Symphony, of "human transformation," albeit a transformation of a very specific kind which I shall attempt to elucidate in due course. First, however, let us pause to consider the Fifth Symphony.

The Symphony No. 5 in C Minor, Op. 67, was composed in 1807. It remains, of course, one of the greatest, most powerful and well-beloved pieces of music ever written. It is tightly organized throughout by the use of recurring rhythmic iterations of the famous four-note opening motif. This motif has been identified with "fate" or "destiny" (and it could even, by further association, be identified with "determinism" as opposed to "free will" or "freedom") but I would submit that it is a symbol of nothing more difficult to understand than "adversity" and that the symphony is simply the musical story of one hero's ultimate triumph over such adversity, whether such "hero" be thought of as a single person, a specific group of people, or the whole of mankind.

In the opening movement, Allegro con brio, the sense of adversity is immediately established with the hammer-blow statement of the four-note motif by two clarinets and the entire string section of the orchestra sounding in powerful double octaves. The constant rhythmic iterations of the motif communicate a sense of the persistence and inevitability of adversity. This impression continues but becomes somewhat softened upon the statement of the second theme, which provides a new feeling of hope such as might arise with the onset of some kind of unexpected assistance in the ongoing struggle to cope with adversity. The feeling of hope immediately disappears at the beginning of the development section as the struggle against adversity intensifies. With the recapitulation, the mood changes to one of utter despair when the oboe intones an expressive and highly plaintive eleven-note rubato solo that produces the effect of an anguished soliloquy of the hero. This brief passage allows the listener momentarily to identify with, and to feel an enormous sympathy for, the hero. The feeling of hope that had been associated with the music of the second theme is now greatly diminished with the restatement of the second theme in the tonic tonality. The feeling quickly dissipates, recalling its sudden disappearance at the beginning of the development section, as the first movement draws to a decisively tragic conclusion.

In the second movement, Andante con moto, the music is such as to communicate to the listener that the hero has found some way to elude the immediacy of catastrophe by finding temporary refuge in some safe place. The music is written in A-flat major, a relative major key of the minor key that opens the symphony. The music is expressed by means of a broad and lovely legato melody that provides a gentle contrast to the stark rhythmic music of the first movement. The melody is structured in two sections and the movement generally may be said to consist of a loose series of variations upon this melody.

The head of the first section of the melody is reminiscent of the legato portion of the second theme of the opening movement—indeed, both melodies commence with an ascending fourth interval—and the sense of a feeling of hope returns, but it is the tail of the first section of the melody that is most remarkable and significant. It consists of an ascending broken A-flat tonic triad in root position that terminates by falling back and coming to a pause upon its second tone.

This motif serves as the germ of that passage of music by which a sense of the triumph over adversity will ultimately be felt—evoking an overwhelming feeling of exhilaration—at the beginning of the fourth movement. This motif is developed, and its symbolism is elucidated, upon the statement of the second section of the melody.

Rhythmic iterations of the four-note "adversity" motif can be heard softly in the strings as a kind of rhythmic counterpoint during the first variation of the second section of the melody. This time, however, the sound of the motif seems to suggest a detached wariness of adversity rather than a frightful exposure to its imminent presence. As the music continues, it seems to suggest that the hero has now begun to think about adversity, to identify the problem that gives rise to it, and to formulate a thorough strategy for solving the problem. A sense of a feeling of increasing heroic self-confidence emerges over the next three variations, which are confined to the first section of the melody: the second variation, in which the melody is given to the violas and cellos; the third, to the first violins; and the fourth, to the cellos and double basses. Through the remainder of the second movement, the music clearly suggests that the hero is refining and completing an effective plan for combatting adversity. With the coda, the listener receives a powerful impression of the hero's firm resolve.

In the third movement, Allegro, the music returns to the original tonality of C minor. It is written as a scherzo and trio, a form which Beethoven invented to structure one of the inner movements (usually the third) of his compositions in sonata form. In general, the scherzo is conspicuously rhythmic, like the minuet of the earlier composers who introduced or adopted the sonata form, but, owing to its liberation from the conventional symbolism of the dance, its access to a wide range of possibilities for musical symbolic expression is considerably enlarged.

The first section of the theme of the scherzo of the Fifth Symphony conveys a profound feeling of mystery. The pitches of the first three tones of the nine-tone head of the first section of the theme are identical with those of the first three tones of the head of the first section of the melody of the slow movement, only they have been transposed from a major tonality to a minor tonality and their rhythmic values and accents have been changed. The import of the micro-symbolism of this music is incontrovertibly clear: the hero has courageously returned to the immediacy of adversity with renewed hope. The four-note rhythmic motif of adversity is heard once again upon the statement of the second section of the theme of the scherzo, signifying a confrontation between the hero and adversity. Two subsequent oscillations between the first and second sections of the theme suggest a running battle during which the hero by turns engages, disengages and reengages with adversity.

The trio of the scherzo is structured as a fugato. Now, in my opinion, the conventional microsymbolism of the fugue signifies rational organization—whether it be man's intellectual organization of knowledge through science and technology or some particular social organization of human beings to accomplish worthy and desirable objectives. Accordingly, the spirited fugato in the third movement of the Fifth Symphony is able to suggest, on the one hand, either a call to arms with active defiance or a call to passive resistance with non-violent protest in a common struggle against social injustice or, on the other hand, an enormous breakthrough in technology that finally enables people to control the impact of natural disasters and to eliminate poverty and disease. Continuing in this line of thinking, for me, the fugato suggests a call both for national democratization among the world's remaining oligarchies and for world federalism among its present democracies in a successful effort to resolve most of the greatest difficulties which still confront mankind.

When the theme of the scherzo resumes following the fugato, the sound of the first section of the theme reminds the listener that the hero is still present but the transformation of the music from arco to pizzicato upon its repeat suggests an atmosphere of increasing mystery. When the four-note motif of adversity is nonchalantly reintroduced in a soft pizzicato passage, the microsymbolism of the music clearly conveys a sense of some kind of an unexpected compromise between the hero and adversity. When the sound of the first section of the theme returns in a legato passage that gradually rises and intensifies as a melodic sequence—one that is clearly reminiscent of the tail of the subject of the fugato—against a bass that proceeds in half steps to turn about and then to rest upon a pedal point on the dominant, the listener comes to apprehend that the hero is no longer subject to adversity, that somehow the hero has established control over adversity, and that adversity has been pacified. With this passage, the third movement concludes in a triumphant *tierce de Picardie* that seamlessly joins the scherzo with the finale.

In the fourth movement, Allegro, the music is written in C major, the parallel major of the original tonality of the symphony. The use of the major tonality and the addition of several new instruments—the piccolo, the contra bassoon and three trombones—permit the four motifs of the finale (namely, the first and second sections of the first and second themes of the exposition) to sound cheerful, bright and majestic. The feeling that is clearly conveyed by all of the motifs is that of triumph over adversity. The first section of the first theme recalls the ending of the first section of the melody of the slow movement. It is music of tremendous joy and strength. This feeling continues with the statement of the second section of the first theme, the beginning of which (like that of the first section) is comprised of a broken C major triad.

The first section of the second theme recalls the four-note rhythmic motif of adversity, only now it is an adversity that seems to have been subjugated and transmuted into an agency of benevolence. It is music of extraordinary self-assurance and self-assertion. This feeling remains unbroken through the statement of the second section of the second theme, the head of which, like that of the first section, consists of a tetrachord, but one descending rather than ascending.

The repeat of the exposition, the presentation of the development (the culmination of which recalls the wondrous amiable transformation of the four-note motif of adversity at the end of the scherzo) and an elaborate treatment of themes in the recapitulation reinforce all of these impressions. The symphony concludes in glorious exhilaration, an effect achieved in the course of the coda by presenting a threefold descending tetrachord (with a momentary hint in the harmonies of the tragedy associated with the original tonality of C minor), each iteration with a strengthening rhythmic intensity and an increasing rate of tempo and volume. After a repetition of the threefold passage, the symphony closes in delirious joy with a brief but stunning reformulation of the opening of the finale.

The Symphony No. 9 in D Minor, Op. 125, was composed in 1823/24. The Ninth Symphony is also known as the Choral Symphony because of the addition of four soloists and a chorus in the final movement to provide a musical rendition of Schiller's poem *To Joy*. Now, because of the symphony's association with extramusical ideas during its climactic movement, it cannot be thought of purely as absolute music. On the other hand, since it proceeds as absolute music throughout three full movements and the instrumental introduction to the fourth movement up to the entrance of the tenor soloist, neither can it be thought of purely as program music. Rather, it is a hybrid of the two kinds of music. Notwithstanding this refinement of classification, it is my sincere hope—subject to the provision that my interpretation of the symbolic meaning of this great symphony can and shall be clearly explained and properly understood—that I may not be judged too harshly for choosing to include the piece in my analyses of macrosymbolism in "seven compositions of absolute music."

Also, in consideration of the unusual length and complexity of this piece, I will strive to focus less upon a detailed structural analysis and more upon my overall impressions of the music.

For me, the Symphony No. 9 is a symbol of natural evolution and of human transformation through the ascendence of reason. It is a symbolic representation—primarily through the medium of music—of the essential ideas of my moral philosophy which I have set forth throughout my previous writings. Briefly stated, this philosophy (which I call *symbiosism* or the ethics of living together) affirms man's evolution from lower forms of life and asserts that man is ever continuing to evolve to a better condition through the ascendence of reason. The ascendence of reason is indicated, on the one hand, through the ascendence and globalization of science and technology and, on the other, through the ascendence of the universal over the particular in human self-awareness and social organization. The present convergence of both tendencies points to a course of world unification in the not-too-distant future. World unification will require a uniform body of legal principles and procedures, supreme among which must be a world constitution with a custodial world court, and depend upon a universal morality predicated upon the principles of non-injury, utility, reciprocity and magnanimity. Allow me now to attempt to outline how the Ninth Symphony suggests to me the essential tenets of symbiosism.

The first movement, Allegro ma non troppo, un poco maestoso, evokes the eras of primordial earth, from the time when the earth first came into being about 4.5 billion years ago through the time of the genesis of life on earth some one billion years later and through that particular time between one and up to ten million years ago when man finally emerged as a distinct genus among the hominoids of the anthropoid primates up to the dawn of civilization. The music evokes a sense of cosmic energy, of savage coldness, of unfathomable mystery.

The second movement, Molto vivace, evokes the ascendence of man. In the scherzo fugato, one can feel the presence of reason and envision early man's unique ability to structure perception, to discover and to utilize knowledge, to introduce and to develop science and technology. With the deliberate repetitions of the theme of the trio (often through sustained pedal points), one can sense the universality of reason.

The third movement, Adagio molto e cantabile, evokes not only a renewed sense of the universality of reason but a fresh sense of the unity of all rational beings. The movement is cast as a set of tender variations upon the most peaceful of melodies and in this music one can sense unity in diversity, can codiscover the origin of human self-awareness and can envisage the practicable probabilities of interpersonal benevolence, of intersocietal cooperation, of world political unification, of universal human well-being, of permanent peace.

The fourth movement, Presto, educes the unification of mankind under the principles of symbiosism. One by one just after the beginning of the movement, the themes that symbolize the initial condition of human life on the earth and either of the subsequent rational antecedents of world sovereignty—the original supremacy of primordial nature; the ascendence of reason as expressed through science and technology; and the ascendence of reason as expressed in a rapidly growing human self-awareness and an emerging sense of universal interdependency—are briefly recalled but quickly dismissed as inimical or inadequate in and of themselves to sustain and to improve human life. The cellos and double basses then introduce the melody of the Ode to Joy, which symbolizes the coming peaceful symbiosist revolution in the ethics and the politics of all peoples. The essence of this ethics is noninjury, utilitarianism and benevolence; of the politics, national democratization and world federalization.

The music of the Ode to Joy proceeds as a set of variations on a theme. It is presented first by the orchestra alone and then by the vocalists in company with the orchestra. A stirring tenor aria cast as an explosively rhythmic variation of the Ode to Joy theme seems to serve as a call for political action. The fugato which follows symbolizes the processes of political organization for national democratization and world federalization. The exuberant restatement of the Ode to Joy music by full chorus and orchestra seems to confirm the ultimate success of the political agenda. A second theme is then presented, a motif from earlier movements that is symbolic of human life or of human self-consciousness and of the most desirable and worthy potentialities of human life and that, in the present context, is highly symbolic of the quest to attain human perfection and of all efforts to develop and to perfect all that is perfectible in human life. The double fugato which follows (in which the Ode to Joy theme is combined in counterpoint with the new theme) symbolizes the endlessness and the interdependency of the processes of human evolution, social progress, and the attainment and maintenance of lifelong personal happiness. The mysterious passages which follow seem to suggest man's endless quest to attain an understanding of the unknowable. The movement then concludes in tremendous jubilation with abbreviated variations on both themes.

In all of my foregoing comments, I have attempted to the best of my ability either to avoid or to minimize an exhaustive analysis of the treatment of themes and motifs throughout the Ninth Symphony. May it suffice now to observe that Beethoven achieves a highly effective aesthetic/symbolic integration in the symphony by the use of but two sets of basic motifs: one, a pair of rising or falling melodic fourths separated by a half step or a whole step moving in the opposite direction, prominent in movements one, three and four and (in my opinion) symbolic of human life, and, two, a movement up and down by step largely within the confines of the interval of the fifth, prominent in movements two and four and (again in my opinion), by means of frequent repetition, effectively symbolic of universality.

The fifth composition which we shall consider is Mendelssohn's Violin Concerto in E Minor, Op. 64. The concerto was written in 1844, three years before the composer's untimely death at the age of 37. It was dedicated to one of Mendelssohn's longtime musical friends, Ferdinand David, who played the solo part for the premiere performance in Leipzig on March 3, 1845. This extraordinary work is one of Mendelssohn's finest musical creations and, at the same time, one of the most beautiful violin concertos ever written. It has always been my favorite of all of the compositions of either category.

The concerto is in three movements (fast-slow-fast) but the first movement is joined to the second and the second to the third with brief interludes which substantially contribute to the macrosymbolism of the concerto as a whole. As it strikes me, this macrosymbolism projects the correlative concepts of grief and consolation. Furthermore, by virtue of the manner by which the instrumentation unfolds, I can gradually discern an almost fully convincing suggestion of some young mother's grief and consolation. The powerful dialectics of this kind of macrosymbolism readily prompts us to classify the macrosymbolism of the concerto within the category of tragicomedy. The beauty which we perceive when we listen to this concerto, like that which we perceive when we listen to either of the two compositions of Mozart that we have previously discussed, symbolically expresses the amiability of compatible relationships. Let us now attempt to follow this story of a young mother's grief and consolation as it proceeds movement by movement through the concerto.

In the opening movement, Allegro molto appassionato, the violin pours out its heart in anguish, as though a young mother has recently learned of the death of one of her children. As the orchestra takes up the music of the opening theme, one senses that everyone whose lives touch that of the young mother shares in her grief. Then the mother continues her sorrowful soliloquy, which seems to conclude with a most tender reflection upon what promises might have been possible had her lost child been able somehow to remain alive.

With the entrance of the second theme against a sustained pedal point by the solo violin (marked *tranquillo* in the score), the clarinets and flutes offer a sincere expression of solace and support, as though the surviving children of the young mother are reacting gently and lovingly to her obvious despair. When the solo violin quickly takes up the same theme, one senses that the mother is responding to the solace provided by her children, that she is beginning to regain some feelings of hope. Such feelings soon cease as again she turns her thoughts to her lost child in passages of music that relentlessly develop the opening theme. Her anguish then intensifies through an impassioned cadenza that reveals her self-perception of emotional isolation. The cadenza culminates with the recapitulation of the opening theme by the full orchestra, during which the solo violin delivers a series of broken chords that sound quite literally like the voice of a broken heart.

Once again, the children seem to be heard in an attempt to offer comfort; once again, the mother seems at first to respond to the solace of the children, afterwards only to be overwhelmed by recurring memories of her loss. As the movement seems to end in tragic despair, a sole bassoon—symbolic perhaps of patience, symbolic perhaps that at least one of the children has not given up his or her seemingly futile attempts to comfort the mother—sustains an isolated tone which eventually rises by a half step to introduce, in company with the other woodwinds and the strings, an unexpected and effectually soothing modulation to the tonality of the middle movement.

In my opinion, Mendelssohn combines four simple musical devices to achieve this serene and uplifting effect. In the first half of the modulation, he allows five of the instrumental parts to enter successively in imitation of the bassoon, each rising by a half step from its initial tone. This melodic motif of a rising minor second in conjunction with the agreeable harmonies richly building up through the counterpoint of the cumulative parts in this very brief quasi-fugato passage produces a clear microsymbol of rational orderliness, of a renewal of hope, of several small but deliberate steps launched toward the healing of a broken heart. In the second half of the modulation, Mendelssohn at first allows the harmonies to move backward, and then to-and-fro, between different positions of the same triad. This gentle treatment of the harmonies in conjunction with a change in meter from the tense alla breve of the opening movement to the more relaxed six-eight time of the middle movement (a meter which composers often use, generally in a moderate tempo, for the composition of barcarolles and lullabies), produces an unmistakable microsymbol of tender and easygoing tranquility.

In the second movement, Andante, the violin sings a beautiful melody of resignation as though the young mother has finally reconciled herself to her loss and, with a recognition that her loss is not hers alone, is setting out from the haven of her home to acknowledge and to reciprocate the consolation of her children. The lullaby character of the music suggests to us that the mother is now gently determined to thank her children for their constant and dependable love, to reassure them that they are healthy and safe, to take up fully once again her various obligations on their behalf. The agitation of the second theme reminds us that the family still is not liberated from disturbing memories, that they still are locked in a difficult struggle to recover from the shock of loss and the pain of grief. This music alternates between expressions by the full orchestra, which now appears to take on the role of a detached narrator, and the solo violin with its supporting ensemble—consisting sometimes of woodwinds and representing the family's occasional anxious dialogue, sometimes only of strings and representing the mother's lingering secret self-reproach. Nonetheless, the return of the beautiful first theme at the close of the movement reassures us that this close family ultimately will rise from the depths of their painful experience and discover a way to become happy together once again.

Our feeling of reassurance intensifies upon hearing the quiet interlude between the second and third movements when the solo violin, accompanied by the string section, makes a gradual modulation to E major, the harmonic major of the original tonality of the concerto. In listening to these three brief passages, we sense that the young mother has finally acquired sufficient strength to cope with her grief, that she will no longer allow it to absorb her thoughts or to drain her vitality, that she is now ready to love life fully once again.

In the first theme of the third movement, Allegro molto vivace, the violin tosses off a light and cheerful melody with the accompaniment of different combinations of the woodwinds as though the young mother and her children have joyfully rejoined the world. An energetic second theme of even greater exuberance seems to reaffirm the power of love and the indomitability of the human spirit. These happy impressions continue and intensify throughout the remainder of the concerto by means of a brief development of the second theme (featuring a new melody based upon an augmentation of the rhythm of the head of the second theme that is presented in turn both by itself and in lovely counterpoint against the first theme and that is evocative in all instances of a sense of restored equanimity and aplomb), a standard recapitulation of both themes, and a delightful coda based upon the heads of both themes.

I have mentioned that the Mendelssohn violin concerto is my favorite violin concerto. Were I to be asked to rank in descending order of preference my five favorite violin concertos, I would be obliged to provide the following list: Mendelssohn, Tchaikowsky, Beethoven, Brahms, Berg. We can see that I have ranked Tchaikowsky second to Mendelssohn on my list and, for more reasons than one, I would like to continue our discussion of macrosymbolism in absolute music by turning to the music of Tchaikowsky. Now, I am confident that a symbolic analysis of the D Major violin concerto should be both highly interesting and abundantly fruitful. Notwithstanding, I am also inclined to believe that an analysis of the B Minor symphony may provide us even greater rewards at this time.

The Symphony No. 6 in B Minor was composed during 1892/93. It was first performed in St. Petersburg on October 28, 1893. Nine days later and in the same city, Tchaikowsky died under somewhat mysterious circumstances at the age of 53. The traditional account of his death states that he intentionally drank unboiled water during an outbreak of cholera while he was experiencing an episode of deep emotional depression. More recent scholarship (through the joint efforts of Alexander Woitov and Alexandra Orlova at the Russian Museum, Leningrad, in 1966) has revealed that a certain influential official in the government of Tsar Alexander II had taken great offense at Tchaikowsky's well-known homosexual relationship with the official's young nephew. This official convened a kind of ad hoc tribunal before which the famous composer was summoned and where he was offered a choice between facing immediate public disclosure with complete personal disgrace or an honorable death by committing suicide with poison. Apparently, Tchaikowsky chose the latter alternative. He was subsequently buried with great honors and his death was attributed to cholera.

The Symphony in B Minor is also generally known by the epithet or subtitle *Pathetique* and it is sometimes considered to be a "program symphony," like Berlioz' Symphonie fantastique and Beethoven's Pastorale Symphony. The sense of sorrow that is felt by the listener throughout so much of the music, interspersed as it is with sections that suggest some sense of diversion and consequential relief, suggest the musical narration of a most unhappy story, such that the macrosymbolism of the symphony clearly must be placed within the category of tragedy. The connotations of the word "pathetique" include sorrow, melancholy, pity, and compassion, and, in company with many other listeners, I would concur that the overall macrosymbolism of the symphony is that of compassion. However, in the following symbolic analysis of the symphony, movement by movement and section by section, I would like to offer my interpretations with respect to the possible meanings of the various microsymbols within an entire series of loosely-related macrosymbols that flow together, from the first quiet phrase of the symphony to the silence that follows the final gently sustained tone, to create the effect of an overall macrosymbolism of compassion.

The first movement, Adagio-Allegro non troppo, evokes the secret inner feelings of an aged man—a man who realizes that he may not have very much longer to live, a man who is fully conscious of all that he has lost, a man who knows that he will neither possess nor experience ever again the things which had brought him so much pleasure and happiness in the past. The movement opens with a slow and languid introduction which conveys a sense of deep depression. After a brief pause, the first theme is introduced—the four-tone head of which is identical (in respect of pitch) to the head of the theme of the introduction—but the fast and energetic presentation conveys an abrupt change of mood to one of acute anguish as though arising from a sudden premonition of impendent death. After a second pause, the second theme is introduced in the relative major key, evoking a feeling of enormous nostalgia for lost vitality. A third theme of graceful character is then introduced in the form of a canon-like duet between the flute and the bassoon. This brief tender exchange suggests a feeling of nostalgia for lost love. The hauntingly beautiful second theme then returns. After a third pause, the music continues with an abrupt change of mood as the development section begins. Inasmuch as the development is based upon the first theme, the sense of acute anguish is felt once again, only this time it feels even more poignant than at first. The music quickly passes to a fugato based upon the four-tone head of the theme, as though the aged man is attempting to discover some kind of rational order underlying his emotional pain but the commencement of the third and fourth statements of the subject of the fugue on the supertonic and submediant respectively (rather than on the tonic and dominant) suggests that reason has given way to emotion. The intensity of the feeling of anguish increases through the course of the development section until it arrives at a climax upon the restatement of the first theme in the recapitulation. At this point, the music provides an impression of heaviness and dissipation (which the composer achieves through the technique of melodic augmentation) and the mood of anguish gradually changes to one of despondency. After a fourth pause, the second theme is heard once again, this time in the parallel major key. Once again, we are moved with a feeling of enormous nostalgia for lost vitality, but this time the feeling of acute anguish does not recur and instead, a peaceful coda suggests a feeling of resignation, of imperturbability, of momentary equanimity.

The feelings of deep nostalgia and consequent regret continue and take on a definite and distinctive quality in each of the three remaining movements.

The second movement, Allegro con grazia, evokes a memory of lost friendship. It is written in quintuple time and in the relative major of the home key of the symphony. Its structure is that of a simple three-part song form with a coda. The lilting primary melody suggests a past time of frequent sociability, of being with one's friends, of attending gatherings and parties, while the melancholy secondary melody suggests a series of plaintive sighs as though to express one's regret for the loss of that which no longer can be.

On the other hand, the third movement, Allegro molto vivace, evokes a memory of lost personal ability. Written as a Scherzo and March (each of which is restated in turn), the music of the scherzo is lively but evanescent, as though the aged man is attempting with little success to recall a time when he possessed a high level of vitality, while the music of the march is assertive, dynamic, and most convincing, as though his memory has at last lucidly congealed around specific past events in his life which involved unquestionable personal accomplishment and honor.

While the symbolic expression of nostalgia and regret for lost friendship is effectually contained within a single movement (the second), that for lost personal ability apparently requires the use of two movements (the third and fourth). The fourth movement, Finale: Adagio lamentoso, evokes the feelings of deep regret and consequent resignation which flow from one's awareness of lost personal ability. The first theme provides a microsymbol of inconsolable grief. It comprises a series of seventh chords (including some diminished seventh chords) that proceed slowly by step in parallel motion to create an effect of bitter lamentation. Tchaikowsky ingeniously increases the impression of emotional agitation by causing the instrumental parts (scored for the strings) to overlap with each other and to proceed, for the most part, not by step but by leap. This masterly technical device at once provides a greater sense of movement and of emotional intensity. (We should note that when the first theme reappears later during the recapitulation, the parts move by step and they no longer overlap. Tchaikowsky thereby allows the lamentation gradually to lose energy and to dissipate during the conclusion.) The second theme provides a microsymbol of noble resignation. It comprises a descending melodic tetrachord and that it is presented as a canon at the octave suggests that the tragic hero no longer is on his own in his painful anguish but has earned the sympathy of all who have become witness to his ordeal. It is presented in the relative major key during the exposition but in the tonic minor during the recapitulation. This subtle shift in tonality, following the mysterious stroke of the gong and a series of solemn soft chords scored for three trombones and a tuba, intensifies the sense of utmost tragedy which prevails throughout the conclusion of the symphony.

Let us recall one more time an aesthetic principle which previously we have attempted to establish, that "the beauty of certain aspects of content which we perceive in a thing of beauty . . . symbolically expresses certain aspects associated with, or conducive to, the orderliness of efficient work and the amiability of compatible relationships." Are we to wonder now how the tragedy of the Sixth Symphony can in any way be symbolic of either of these two necessary and characteristic experiences of human life? Admittedly, the question is among the most difficult which we have raised. Let us attempt to answer it in this manner: if the symphony is a macrosymbol of compassion, then it must be concerned with the amiability of compatible relationships. As we listen to the symphony, we feel compassion for the tragic hero—we share in his nostalgia, we feel his anguish, we admire his courage. We are left with a comfortable consciousness that if we can have such feelings for this tragic hero, perhaps others will have similar feelings for any of us who should ever experience tragic misfortune.

The last composition which we shall consider is Rachmaninoff's Symphony No. 2 in E Minor. During the last years of the Romanov Dynasty, at about the turn of the century, three great composers emerged in Russia: Alexander Scriabin, Igor Stravinsky, and Sergei Rachmaninoff. Scriabin and Stravinsky quickly entered new and different directions with their music; Rachmaninoff alone remained to uphold the musical tradition of Tchaikowsky and to become the last of the great Russian Romanticists.

Rachmaninoff's Second Symphony, like Tchaikowsky's Sixth, expresses a deep sense of pathos. However, the story which it relates is unlike that of the Tchaikowsky symphony: it is an epic, not a tragedy. As in the Tchaikowsky symphony, it is the end of the story—as narrated in the fourth movement—that is critical in determining whether the story of the symphony should be classified as an epic or a tragedy. Again, as in the Tchaikowsky symphony, the symbolism of the music which we are about to consider may be said to be primarily concerned with the amiability of compatible relationships, but this time, it will be far less difficult for us to recognize how this should be so.

I would like to remind my readers that the interpretation of this music which I am about to offer is highly subjective and I am willing to acknowledge that there may be some, perhaps many, who will entirely disagree with it. Nevertheless, I would like to relate my candid personal impressions of the music and, hopefully, to provide a respectable and plausible interpretation of its symbolism.

To me, the music of Rachmaninoff's Second Symphony—like that of Tchaikowsky's Sixth—is a kind of musical interior monologue. In the Second Symphony, we are listening to the story of a person who has experienced an overwhelming personal loss and, in this person's mind, the loss is entirely or largely attributable to the person's past misdeeds. The person expresses remorse and offers an apology to some unknown other (or others) who has (or have) been hurt but we never learn whether this apology was ever accepted. We do become aware that the person then feels a sense of relief and that this feeling is followed with a renewal of self-esteem by virtue of the person's deliberate and unilateral act of asking for pardon. Accordingly, the overall theme of the macro-symbolism of the Second Symphony may be said to be remorse with subsequent self-purification through an offer of an apology. Without engaging in the same kind of formal analysis of this music as I have in most of my previous interpretations of the symbolism of the music of selected symphonies and concertos, I would like now simply to offer my personal impressions and symbolic interpretation of each of the four movements of the symphony.

The first movement, Largo; Allegro moderato, evokes an increasing sense of loss and an emerging feeling of remorse. The music is punctuated with reminiscences—some rather opaque, even dreamy, and others quite vivid. Feelings of constant sorrow deepen as the music progresses. The intense subjectivity of the music—which conveys some sense of the expression of a secret autobiography—is heightened through the brief and very quiet sounds of various solo instruments (occasionally unaccompanied) such as the English horn, the clarinet, and the violin. Near and at the end of the movement, the music evokes an acutely painful sense of loss, of mental agitation, of inescapable self-reproach.

The second movement, Allegro molto, conveys a sense of nostalgia. At the beginning, the music alternates between lively passages which reminisce upon past joy and a slower contemplative passage that longs for a happiness which is no longer possible. In the middle of the movement, an energetic fugato reminisces upon past activity, imparting a sense of rational direction, of a purpose for (with a corollary commitment to) one's life, of tireless personal ambition. The music then continues with a reiteration of the passages which were heard at the beginning of the movement, invoking more nostalgic reminiscences and hopeless yearnings. At the very end, the nagging sense of loss returns accompanied by a feeling of bitter frustration.

The third movement, Adagio, opens with soft passages from the string section which suggest persistent feelings of nostalgia. Against this melancholy backdrop, a solo clarinet delivers one of the most beautiful melodies ever created in the literature for this instrument, an elegy of self-reproach, remorse, and apology. Toward the final tones of the melody, at the point where it would seem to be unequivocally logical to bring the musical narrative to a close because all that had been necessary to say has already been said, the clarinet repeats the concluding phrase, not just once but twice, like a guilty person who, in begging forgiveness of another, cannot stop after a single supplication but must continue to ask over and over again.

The orchestra continues with soft passages which evoke the utmost poignancy of a sense of loss that has been with us since the beginning of the symphony. But as the music progresses, the listener suddenly senses that the protagonist has finally succeeded in detaching reason from emotion—as though through one's act of asking for forgiveness, one has learned how to forgive oneself—thereby attaining some measure of personal equanimity.

The Adagio concludes with unison strings taking up the opening elegiac melody while other instruments provide a nostalgic counterpoint largely comprised of the soft introductory phrases of the movement. A brief coda evokes a sense of ultimate resignation and self-composedness.

The fourth movement, Allegro vivace, conveys a discrete sense of self-purification. Projecting sounds and arousing emotions hitherto unheard and unfelt in the symphony, the first theme is filled with vitality, joy, and hope. A marchlike second theme suggests optimistic determination before the music enters into a jubilant repetition of the first theme.

Then, a slower section (for the most part over a pedal point) conveys once again a mood of optimistic determination, but this time, the feeling seems far more pronounced than when it was first expressed. The music continues with fleeting reminiscences of the introductory passages of the Adagio but the feelings of nostalgia which are consequently reawakened no longer seem quite like the hopeless yearnings of the previous movement.

The music next returns to the mood of optimistic determination and an excitement is generated which is gradually increased through the presence of a prolonged series of deliberate descending scales. Emotional tension is also created and gradually intensified through an alternating juxtaposition of the passages which give rise to optimistic determination with melancholy passages which seem to reminisce unyieldingly on all that has been lost from the past. Notwithstanding, the unrelenting spirit of optimism prevails and the music passes on triumphantly to a restatement of the themes which were heard at the beginning of the movement. The finale (and the symphony) then concludes with music of undiminished joy that conveys the various feelings of increasing optimism, of a renewal of self-esteem, and of the ultimate triumph of goodness.

With these brief comments on the symbolic meaning of the Rachmaninoff Second Symphony, we bring to a close our subjective analyses of macrosymbolism in absolute music. If some of my readers should question why I have limited this discussion to selected works from the symphonic repertoire of particular German and Russian composers, I would argue that the greater number of the works of the greater number of Italian and French composers must properly be classified as program music of one kind or another: the high mass, the masque, the madrigal, the chanson, the opera, the suite, the ballet, the symphonic poem. The same may be said of the music of the various composers of the national movement in nineteenth century and early twentieth century music: the music of these composers, with few exceptions, must properly be classified as program music. Even in German music, we readily acknowledge that much of the music of Johann Sebastian Bach and George Frederick Handel—and almost all of the output of Richard Wagner and Richard Strauss—also must properly be classified as program music.

For final thoughts, I would like to acknowledge the use of form in absolute music as the most effective means to provide a symbol of the rational organization of useful work or of the stability and dependability of symbiotic interpersonal relationships. The powerful effect of a well-conceived formal structure to support the content of artistic expression is the same in music as in painting and architecture or literature and drama. Furthermore, I would like to acknowledge the supremacy of tonal or diatonic music—music which is derived from, and organized about, the natural harmonics or overtones that are emitted (as supplements to the fundamental tone that is always produced) upon the vibration of any elastic body. This kind of music received its earliest complete development through the efforts of Johann Sebastian Bach and reached the epitome of its expression in the music of Wolfgang Amadeus Mozart. Now, I believe that the reason that the music of Mozart appears (at least in our own time) to attract the greatest number of admirers among those who profess to enjoy fine music is that it clearly represents that kind of music that most closely approaches the obvious beauty of natural sound. Consequently, I expect that the music of Mozart will continue to be the most universally beloved among all of the various kinds of music for as long as human life endures.

EPILOGUE

Truth is central to any clear understanding of human existence or of everyone's quest for personal happiness inasmuch as in its absence we live with endless illusion while our survival is ever precarious and our happiness generally short-lived. With truth, we become able to understand the cosmos, the world within the cosmos, and our own unique biosphere within the world. Of even greater importance for the attainment and preservation of our personal happiness, we become able to understand ourselves—whether as members of a single unifiable species, as members of discrete functional groups, or as differentiated unique individuals.

Both knowledge and goodness have their origin in truth; it is the foundation of science and ethics. All that we can learn to enable us to satisfy the necessities of life, to overcome the problems that threaten human existence, and to build a better world is provided to us, or obtained for us, through the product of all of the various sciences. All that we can learn to enable us to live together in peace for our mutual survival and well-being is provided to us, or obtained for us, through the contribution of ethics. However, we would do well if we were now to acknowledge, and henceforth always to remember, that ethics precedes science: if it were not so, knowledge would eventually fall into the hands of evil, providing a benefit for the few while inflicting a detriment upon the many.

There may be some who would interpose now to give voice to the statement that goodness precedes knowledge. This statement appears to reflect the import of the mythological story of the Garden of Eden. However, the story of the tree of the knowledge of good and evil is not the progeny of reason but of imagination. The narrative of the evolution of the human species is not a story of the fall of Adam but of the rise of Everyman. Is it not true that our experience most clearly demonstrates to us that it is impossible to be good without first learning how to be good? To state that goodness precedes knowledge, then, is to prevaricate. Only the reverse statement can be true, that knowledge precedes goodness, but it is knowledge of a certain kind: the knowledge of how to be good. It is for this reason that we can say that ethics precedes science. Ethics creates goodness and goodness identifies that condition under which knowledge can never be deliberately misapplied or abused. With goodness, a goodness such as that that can be easily disseminated throughout the world through the service of a universal morality, human existence will become secure and stable, and then it will soon become possible for everyone everywhere to seek, to attain, and to sustain a pleasant and happy life.

Human perfection identifies that condition in which each person not only successfully satisfies all of the requirements for his or her existence (while, at the same time, each person successfully averts or counteracts the hurts of, or dangers to, his or her existence) but achieves so great a degree of awareness of his or her success as to attain and to sustain the highest possible degree of pleasure and happiness in life. Beauty is a representation of perfection, particularly that of human existence. Our experience of beauty enables us at once to relieve our anxiety and distress and to increase our pleasure and happiness. The experience of beauty also enables us to recognize the circumstances of perfect human existence and of optimal interpersonal conduct. The experience of beauty, then, both increases our pleasure and happiness and enables us to envision an ideal of human life and behavior. The latter effect assists us in establishing and developing an effective methodology by which we can strive toward perfection, that is, it enables us to conceive, to formulate, and to implement an appropriate ethics to achieve—in concert with all of the sciences—the optimization of human well-being. The satisfaction of our needs and the mitigation or elimination of our hurts are impossible to achieve without truth and goodness, but the perception of beauty, and particularly the cognitive awareness of the moral values communicated through the symbolism of works of artistic beauty, increase our self-awareness, pleasure and happiness. Accordingly, the experience of the beauty of nature and of art will always be a part of the good life for as long as human life endures.

The experience of religion is another matter. When the world of man was entirely subject to the law of nature—long before the rapid ascendence of the law of reason—man sought to escape from the terrors of life and the mystery of death by taking refuge in the creations of his imagination. Thus religion soon after came into being to provide solace, comfort and hope. However, with the continuous development of his rational faculties, man gradually became able to overcome the exigencies of nature. Through reason alone—without the necessity of waiting until he may have acquired through natural selection the anatomical perfection of, say, a tiger or a shark—man became able to eliminate his predators. Through reason alone, man became able as well to obtain or to create the wherewithal to meet the necessities of life. Through reason alone, man is finally becoming able now to work together as members of a common species to acquire the knowledge and the resources to optimize the well-being of the species and the happiness of each person. Through all of this cultural progress, the role of religion has so changed that it no longer assists but imperils human survival.

The three crucial problems which we are now clearly able to associate with and to attribute to religion include: (1) the actuality of and the potentiality for catastrophic religious warfare; (2) the persistent presence of a collective subjectivity that is neither objective nor rational but divisive; and (3) an endless suspension of mystery or uncertainty that at once permits the emergence and fosters the continuance of bad faith in personal attitudes and interpersonal conduct. For all of these reasons, whether they be considered separately or in combination, we are able only to conclude: (1) that religion is quickly becoming obsolete; (2) that, paradoxically, its continuing presence in human affairs is becoming increasingly inimical to human well-being and happiness; and (3) that it must ultimately perish before it brings about a universal subversion of reason and the self-destruction of a species.

As we pass through the first decade of the twenty-first century, we find ourselves in an increasingly complex world. We talk about the United States as the sole superpower but it is clear that its power and influence have decided limits. We talk about the United Nations as a body corrupt that is in urgent need of drastic reform. We talk about the United Kingdom as a nation muddling along, of the fiction of the Commonwealth of Nations, of the loss of a great empire. We talk about the European Union as the first supranational sovereignty of democratic nations but we can see how difficult it has been for Europe to arrive at any semblance of consensus and we fear that its emergence as a unified political entity will only serve to prolong racism in the world as it is perceived by the other nations primarily to advance an agenda of self-interest. We talk about national democratization but we forget that virtue resides in the democracy and not in the nation. We talk about the triumph of international capitalism in a new global economy but we witness increasing injury and injustice in an unregulated and essentially lawless economic environment. We talk about China as the only significant power to remain after the fall of communism and, with great astonishment and some degree of concern, we watch it adapt, grow and thrive. We talk about the third world, about its considerable ignorance and poverty, and in particular we observe with great apprehension the rise of Islamic extremism and its misguided efforts to restore and then to expand a lost caliphate. We talk about the ascendence of reason in the modern world, of the globalization of technology, of the increasing potential for world unification and the emergence of a universal morality but when we look around us at any present moment, we see only a world habitually divided and hopelessly unreconciled. Nonetheless, for those of us whose minds are most clear and whose wills are most strong, this sense of irony will serve not to nourish despair but to illuminate a roadbed into the future of our dreams. Once we have seen the light of reason, we can do nothing other than to keep it alight and to walk constantly where it points us.

Imagination has failed mankind, imagination and all of its fruits, except wherever reason has rescued it or wherever it has been in the direct service of reason. The moral education of the young must be liberated from religion and henceforth entrusted to public education. Furthermore, moral education must become the foundation of the education of every human being. These momentous reforms in education must take place in every democracy to improve the quality of life of each person in every society of the human species. Every principle and precept of public and private morality must be thoroughly rational and unequivocally communicable. Furthermore, the systems of public education and criminal justice must be so integrated in every democratic society that each human being without exception can learn how to be agreeable, useful and happy. This last statement infers that ongoing public moral education—including both remedial education and psychiatric healthcare wherever either need should be identified during a preliminary assessment of the criminal between the times of conviction and sentence—becomes the new foundation of criminal punishment. The ultimate effect of these changes in public policy will be a substantial general improvement in human well-being that is at present almost unimaginable.

At the same time, the democracies of the world must quickly unite into a world federation to unify the human species, to save mankind from self-extinction, and to optimize the quality of human life everywhere. All morals and legislation throughout the jurisdictions of the nascent world democratic federal government must be essentially rational. Furthermore, all of the legislation and all of that portion of the morals that effect the general security of person, property and the biosphere must be objective so that they can be comprehended and upheld by every member of the world society. While all of this is happening, national democratization among the various remaining oligarchies of the world must continue to proceed so that new democracies can continue to emerge to join the world federation until it shall have so increased in size with respect to land area, population and number of nations as to comprise the majority of the habitable land, nations and peoples of the world. Once this has happened, the evolution of our species and the history of mankind will have entered a new era, an era of unprecedented personal success and social progress, an era of enduring social stability and personal happiness—the golden age of Earth.

The golden age of Earth will be an age of enlightenment without end. At once, it will be the age of the Dionysian Deposition and the Apollonian Succession. It will be the zenith of the age of the law of reason.

During the golden age of Earth, the human species will be unified into a single family. All people will be members of a universal society. All people will be citizens of the world democratic federal government. All people will live under a common body of laws. All people will be bound by a common morality. Warfare will be abolished. International aggression will disappear. Crime will be eliminated along with poverty and disease. Knowledge will have no boundaries and technology will flourish.

During the golden age of Earth, human life will be long and happy, filled with learning, accomplishment and meaning. Each person will live the good life in good faith and with goodwill. Each person will be able to achieve complete self-realization. No person who seeks will fail to find love.

During the golden age of Earth, every child will be wanted and loved. No child will fail to receive a thorough and an effectual education. No child will be ignored or neglected. No child will be unhappy.

During the golden age of Earth, every elderly person will be honored and respected. No elderly person will fail to receive adequate healthcare or an income sufficient to maintain subsistence. No elderly person will fail to live a long and happy life and to obtain a peaceful and painless death.

During the golden age of Earth, goodness will engender security and stability; truth, pleasure and happiness; and beauty, an increase in, and an intensification of, pleasure and happiness. All roads lead to the future but only one road leads directly to the golden age of Earth. Let us now depart together to gain our entrance to it, and then let us proceed together upon it until we shall have arrived at where we long to be.

BIBLIOGRAPHY

Bentham, Jeremy. *The Principles of Morals and Legislation*. Amherst, N.Y.: Prometheus Books, 1988.

Freud, Sigmund. *Moses and Monotheism*. Standard Ed., 23. New York: Random House, 1967.

Horace. *Satires, Epistles, and Ars Poetica*. Cambridge, Mass.: Harvard University Press, 1926.

Locke, John. *An Essay Concerning Human Understanding*. New York: Oxford University Press, 1979.

Locke, John. *Two Treatises of Government*. Student Ed. Cambridge: Cambridge University Press, 1988.

Mill, John Stuart. *Utilitarianism*. Amherst, N.Y.: Prometheus Books, 1987.

Newton, Isaac. *Principia*. Amherst, N.Y.: Prometheus Books, 1995.

Pascal, Blaise. *Les Pensées*. Indianapolis, Ind.: Hackett Publishing Company, 2005.

Sartre, Jean-Paul. *Being and Nothingness*. New York: Washington Square Press, 1992.

Taylor, Charles Thomas. *Symbiosism*. Lanham, Maryland: Hamilton Books, 2006.

Tylor, Edward B. *Primitive Culture*. 6th Ed. New York: Putnam's Sons, 1920.

LIST OF ARTISTIC WORKS CITED

1812 Overture (Tchaikowsky, P.), 49
Children on the Seashore at Guernsey (Renoir), 44
Clarinet Concerto in A Major, K622 (Mozart, W. A.), 54
Concerto for Flute and Harp in C Major, K299 (Mozart, W. A.), 53-55
Concerto for Violin and Orchestra (Berg, A.), 66
Crime and Punishment (Dostoyevsky, F.), 47
Die Meistersinger von Nürnberg (Wagner, R.), 50
Don Quixote (Cervantes, M. de), 51
Don Quixote (Strauss, R.), 51
Ein Heldenleben (Strauss, R.), 51
Guernica (Picasso), 44, 46
Joseph Being Sold by his Brothers (Overbeck), 46
La Bohème (Puccini, G.), 49
Madame Bovary (Flaubert, G), 47
Madame Butterfly (Puccini, G.), 49
No Exit (Sartre, J-P.), 20
Pictures at an Exhibition (Mussorgsky, M.), 43, 50
Remembrance of Things Past (Proust, M.), 47
St. George and the Dragon (Raphael), 45
Siddhartha (Hesse, H.), 48
Silas Marner (Eliot, G.), 31
Symphonie fantastique (Berlioz, H.), 49, 67
Symphony No. 5 in C Minor (Beethoven, L. Van), 58-62
Symphony No. 6 in F Major (Beethoven, L. Van), 49, 67
Symphony No. 9 in D Minor (Beethoven, L. Van), 58, 62-64
Symphony No. 27 in G Major, K. 199 (Mozart, W. A.), 44
Symphony No. 39 in E Flat Major, K 543 (Mozart, W. A.), 55-58
Symphony No. 40 in G Minor, K. 550 (Mozart, W. A.), 55
Symphony No. 41 in C Major, K. 551 (Mozart, W. A.), 55
Symphony No. 2 in E Minor (Rachmaninoff, S.), 69-71

INDEX OF GENERAL SUBJECTS

absolute, 48, 52-72
program, 48, 62, 71, 72
tonal, 72
Mythology, 16, 20, 73

Narrator, musical, 50, 51, 58, 66
National democratization, 4, 61, 75, 76
Nature, 5, 6, 13, 14, 19, 20, 27, 39, 41, 42, 74 (see also Human nature)
Nature, law of, 2, 5, 6, 19, 27, 41, 74
New covenant, the, 26, 27
Nirvana, 22, 24, 25, 48 (see also Samsara)

Objectivity, 20, 29-31, 33, 36, 75 (see also Truth)
Optimality, 29, 40, 74

Pain, 2, 4, 5, 7, 10, 13, 37
Paradise, 19
Pascal's Wager, 10, 40
Perfectibility, human, 28, 34, 74 (see also Perfection, existential)
Perfection, 8, 11, 19, 20, 28, 29, 34, 38, 41-43, 74
existential, 19, 28, 29, 34, 38, 42, 43, 74 (see also Perfectibility, human)
Platonic didacticism (see Art, function of: didactic)
Pleasure, 2, 4-10, 13, 74, 77
Polytheism, 33 (see also Gods and goddesses)
Public policy, 76

Reason, 2, 4-10, 13, 14, 16, 18-20, 27-29, 32, 39, 40, 62, 74-76
Reason, law of, 2, 3, 19, 74, 76
Religion, v, vi, 6-11, 13-40, 74, 75

as a cause of bad faith, 36-39, 75
as a cause of war, 35, 36, 39, 75
as a cause of world disunity, 36, 39, 75
philosophy of, 11
Romanticism, 31, 32

Sacrificial love, 25-27
Samsara, 24, 48 (see also Nirvana)
Saoshyant, 18 (see also Messiah and Savior)
Satan, 18, 19, 40
Savior, 18, 26, 33, 34 (see also Messiah and *Saoshyant*)
Science, 73, 74 (see also Scientific technology, ascendence and globalization of)
Scientific technology, ascendence and globalization of, 3, 4, 19, 34, 62, 75, 76 (see also Science)
Self-awareness, 4, 32, 39
Self-deception, 9, 32, 38
Self-definition, 32
Self-realization, 32, 33, 40, 76
Self-reliance, 29, 34
Sheol, 19 (see also *Arallû* and Hades)
Social contract, 4
Soma, 21 (see also *Haoma*)
Son of God, the, 25, 26
Spirits, 14-16, 18, 19, 39, 40
transmigration of, 15, 16
Stoicism, 22
Subjectivity, 20, 32, 33, 36, 37, 75
Suffering, 23, 24, 37 (see also Misery)
Supernatural, the, 6-9, 14-16, 29, 33-35, 39, 40
Symbolism, v, vi, 8, 9, 11, 20, 21, 30, 31, 42-72

as a symbolic representation of
amiable relations, vi, 43,
53-58, 64-72
as a symbolic representation of
effective work, vi, 43, 54,
58-64, 72
conventional, 20, 21, 30, 31,
45, 46
in the form of macrosym-
bolism, 30, 31, 46, 47, 52-
71
in the form of microsym-
bolism, 30, 46-51, 67-69
nonconventional, 20, 21, 45,
46

Tartarus (see Hell)
Ten Commandments, the, 26, 35
Theism, 33, 39
Tonal music, 72
Torah, the, 26
Tragedy, 44, 52, 53, 67-69
Tragicomedy, 64-66
Truth, 10, 19, 23, 24, 29-33, 40, 48,
73, 74, 77 (see also Objec-
tivity)
empirical evidence, 30, 31 (see
also Empiricism)
real, 31
representational fidelity, 30, 31

subjective authenticity, 30-33
verbal, 31

Universal compassion, 25-27
Universal democratic society (see
World democratic federal
government)
Universal morality, 19, 36, 75, 76
Universal respect for all sentient
beings, 29
Universalism, ascendence of
over particularism, 4, 62, 75,
76
Utilitarianism, 4, 5, 31
Utility, 24, 42

Veda, the, 21 (see also Avesta, the)
Visual arts (see Art, spatial)

Wisdom, Lord of, 22, 27, 33, 34
World democratic federal govern-
ment, 4, 36, 76
World federalization, 4, 61, 76
World peace, 19, 36, 48
World unification, 76

Yoga, 24

Zoroastrianism, 17, 18, 21, 22

INDEX OF PROPER NAMES

INDEX OF SYMBOLS

ABOUT THE AUTHOR

Charles Thomas Taylor was born in 1941 in Orange, New Jersey. His earliest interests centered about classical music and by age nineteen, he had mastered piano and organ. After a number of years of teaching music to private pupils, he earned an undergraduate degree in business administration at La Salle University of Philadelphia, Pennsylvania, graduating magna cum laude in 1971. He was introduced to philosophy while a student at La Salle and he wrote his first book, *The Values*, within a four-month period immediately following his final studies there. *The Values*, a concise work of contemporary ethics, was published in 1977 by Philosophical Library of New York.

Since 1976, Mr. Taylor has been a resident of Colorado, working in the field of accounting. He is presently the Director of Finance at Airport Development Group, Inc., a small engineering and consulting firm in Denver, Colorado. He holds an M.B.A. and an M.S. in finance from the University of Colorado (1995) and became a C.P.A. in Colorado in 1997. He wrote his second book of moral philosophy, *Person and Society*, in 1998. This book was published two years later by Pentland Press of Raleigh, North Carolina.

During the eight years that have passed since he wrote his second book, Mr. Taylor has completed three additional books of philosophy in the areas of politics, ethics, religion and art. *Toward World Sovereignty*, which examines the benefits and problems associated with the vision of creating a universal democratic federal government, was published in 2002 by University Press of America of Lanham, Maryland. *Symbiosism*, which addresses the challenge of formulating a uniform and practicable universal morality that might serve as a model for a world that otherwise shall have attained in the future some semblance of political and economic integration, was published in 2006 by Hamilton Books of Lanham, Maryland. The present book, which considers the relevance of religion and art within the ethical and political context of his previous writings, was completed in December, 2005.

Mr. Taylor is currently at work on a sixth book that highlights the necessity of strengthening and expanding moral education in all of the democratic socie-

ties of the world, not only within the traditional education of children and young people but also for the successful rehabilitation of all persons convicted of crime or diagnosed with mental illness.